MONEY SMARTS

MONEY SMARTS

What Students Want, Graduates Need, and Parents Wish To Know About Money

NATHAN NGUYEN

MONEY SMARTS
What Students Want, Graduates Need, and Parents Wish to Know
About Money

by NATHAN NGUYEN

ISBN 978-0-9992727-1-8 (paperback)
ISBN 978-0-9992727-4-9 (Epub)
Library of Congress Control Number: 2017911949

DEDICATED to my family, who have been the greatest source of strength for me along my journey, and without whom none of this would be possible. And to my mentors and students who continue to challenge and inspire me to become better every day.

TABLE OF CONTENTS

INTRODUCTION

EVERY YEAR MILLIONS OF STUDENTS graduate high school and begin their exciting journey to adulthood. So how do most of them start? Naturally, by claiming their freedom and independence through passing a driving test and getting their driver's license. With license in hand, the student is no longer a passenger. He is now in the driver's seat, in control of his car and his life. But wait. Let's just imagine for a moment that there is no license exam or a driving test. There won't be any written exam to ensure that he knows the rules of driving and no driving test to make sure that he has the skills to operate his car. By high school graduation, he is given a car along with some basic instructions and off he goes. He will learn how to drive as he drives. In the process, he hopes that he won't kill anyone or get killed. Sound ridiculous?

Well, that's exactly what is happening with money today. Students enter adulthood with little to no money knowledge and skills. Young adults are financially unprepared and yet are expected to financially succeed somehow.

The world is changing – and the world of money is changing even faster. If people were confused before about how money worked, they are going to be completely lost with the rise of global trade and the financial integration of the world economy. What does this mean for students? If they want to succeed financially, it will take more than book smarts – they will also need Money Smarts. The question to think about is, how can students, graduates, or anyone be expected to succeed financially without money knowledge and skills?

The ways of making money, spending money, investing money, and borrowing money have all changed. Anybody can work anywhere for anyone and get paid instantly at any time. A person can work from home and even make money while he sleeps. Spending money can involve just a few simple mouse clicks, and products can be delivered to the front door within hours. People can even spend money they don't have with instant credit decisions and monthly payment financing options. There are more investment opportunities than there are people to invest in them. Company valuations have never been higher – investors today value companies who may be loosing money or even haven't produced any profits at billions of dollars. Money is borrowed in just a few clicks, and instant credit accounts are created for immediate use. This is just the tip of the iceberg. As the money system keeps on advancing with complexity, it is up the people to keep up with the changes. For those who do, these changes can mean great wealth opportunities.

This is how I was able to become a millionaire at age 23 while going to college full time. I made $4.3 million dollars within 24 months and completed my bachelor's degree in Business Administration from the University of Southern California. Since then I have generated many more millions over the past decade using the Money Smarts that you will learn in this book. My story was featured in the all-time bestselling Chicken Soup for the Soul series book *Chicken Soup for the Extraordinary Teens Soul* as well as *The Richest Kids in America*. I am also a frequent guest on national and local TV, radio, and media publications sharing my story and have been hired to speak, lecture, and train people on money, success, and strategic planning.

Can you do this? Absolutely! And if I fulfilled my mission with this book, you can do it even better. You don't need permission, a particular status, or be a certain age. Beyond your desire and commitment to taking action, all you need are money knowledge and skills. If you are feeling discouraged because you feel that you don't have enough to start, don't be. I know what it feels like to start with little or nothing. It is actually irrelevant. I have learned that success is built more on resourcefulness than resources.

I was only five years old when I came to America with my family as refugees from Vietnam. As a family of eight, we started on welfare and food stamps from the government. While we had little to no money, we believed in the American Dream and that America was the land of endless opportunities for big dreams to come true. We knew it wasn't going to be easy, but at least we were given a chance. We were all hopeful.

Among the big hopes was me doing well in school. While I tried, I didn't make my family very proud when I immediately failed. I am proof that you can actually fail kindergarten! The only reason I passed kindergarten on my second year trying was that the school made my brother sit with me for the whole year (forcing him, in turn, to repeat first grade). While I advanced grade by grade each year because I got older, I did not learn well. In seventh grade, all students had to take a standardized test to judge their academic level. Well, as it turns out, I was reading at a first-grade level. That explained why I was struggling in other subjects. I was put in English Language Development classes and other specialized electives that offered me extra help to catch up with the others.

When it was time to apply for college, my SAT was in the lowest percentile, breaking 1000 points on a 1600 point scale. When asked what I wanted to do, I wasn't clear other than I wanted to be like my mentors, mostly business people who served on boards of directors for nonprofits helping the community.

When I filled out my Free Application for Federal Student Aid (FAFSA), my Estimated Family Contribution was zero-my family had no money for me to go to college. I needed to depend on scholarships, student loans, student work study, and government aid to earn my degree. I knew that while the cost of going to college was high, the opportunity cost of not going to college was much higher. So I was determined to go to college and fund my way.

Knowing that I needed to rely on myself to pay for school, I applied to many scholarships early, and these paid for my degree. Among the scholarships I received, the Horatio Alger National Scholarship had the most profound impact on me. Not only did it give me $10,000 (at the time of writing, it is now up to $25,000 and increasing), it also gave me something more valuable: my mentor, Mark Victor Hansen, who along with other members of the Horatio Alger Association inspired me to become an entrepreneur and investor. As it turns out, with my businesses and investments, I ended up not needing the full $10,000 scholarship, so the remainder was left back for the Association to help other students.

When I received the Horatio Alger National Scholar award in 2004, I also met John Paul DeJoria, the self-made billionaire known for Paul Mitchell hair products and Patron tequila, who shared with me that "success without sharing is failure." I took that to heart. It's clear that my mission is to help other students realize their unlimited potential and assist them to achieve more than they thought possible for themselves. If you are a student reading this book, I am excited for what you will accomplish with this, so I challenge you to pay it forward so that the next generation will be better than the next and so forth.

If money is a game, you now have in your hands the money playbook. When you read this book and absorb its lessons, you will be able to play the money game and not get played by the game. You will learn the different aspects of money and how each relates to the others. In the end, you will understand money. You will learn how to create the financial freedom you want and have the strategies to achieve it.

My only advice for how to get the most of this book is to read it thoroughly without skipping any chapters. The concepts build on each other. I am confident that when you put into practice these Money Smarts learned from this book, I will soon be reading your success story!

Chapter One
GET INTO THE GAME

Life begins when you get out of the grandstand and into the game.-P. L. Debevoise

ACROSS AMERICA AND AROUND THE world, sports are part of our culture and tradition. Generation after generation, we encourage our children to play sports and get into the game. It doesn't matter if our kids become professional athletes or not. It just matters that they get involved rather than sitting on the bench and be spectators for the rest of their lives.

Money is just the same. It doesn't matter if the student pursues a career in finance or business to need to learn it. If money is a game, it is a game that everyone will need to play. Regardless if people are prepared for it or not, they will be put into the game. What this means is that everyone should need to learn about money if they want to do well. Just like any game player, don't just sit on the bench or allow yourself to get benched. Get into the game as much and as early as possible to practice to have the best chance of winning.

But this is not happening. Currently, students are being benched and are not given much opportunity to get into the game of money. Often, students are protected and shielded from financial responsibility so they can focus on academics. Thus, when students graduate high school and begin adulthood, the transition from little to no responsibility to becoming an independent adult is difficult. It is also during this time that students make key life decisions that can dramatically affect their futures, such as selecting and paying for college, choosing what to study, and all the other financial decisions including car loans and credit cards. As a new adult after high school, these are big decisions to make. When it is too difficult for these students to make decisions, they have others make decisions for them (their parents by default), and thus, many students stay on the bench throughout college. Although age makes them legally adults, they don't have the confidence to be adults truly.

When college ends, and the reality of life shines through, many college graduates struggle to be on their own.

The reality for these unprepared new adults is not great. When students graduate college, only one in three has the key work experience they need to succeed.[1] According to a PayScale survey, only 25% of recent grads felt they were "extremely prepared" for their new jobs while yet only 8% of managers agreed.[2] Many new graduates are shocked at how competitive it is to get the job they want, and they settle for lesser quality jobs that are unrelated to their college study. This is called being underemployed, which is better than being unemployed because it still earns money to pay for financial obligations, but it is a big surprise to many graduates.

For those who are unemployed altogether, it is easy to blame the economy for the lack of opportunities. However, few will admit that the problem isn't the lack of opportunities but rather their lack of preparation to qualify for the opportunities available. I recently met Walter Scott Jr., a billionaire businessman and investor and asked him for his secret to success. His answer was, "finding good people." He further emphasized that he was "always looking for good people." What this means is that the demand for good people is always there, but just not enough people to fill them. It is important for graduates to understand that if they want to achieve greatness, they first need to become "great". My father once shared with me that I should "never worry about if I can get a job or not but rather worry about if I can do the job or not."

If graduates take on a lot of student loans and don't develop their skills in addition to getting their college degree, they can end up underemployed and join the half of Americans that are living paycheck to paycheck.[3] Living paycheck to paycheck means that every penny of every check is spent, and workers are not able to save. Recent data shows that half of working-age households have zero saved in retirement accounts, and of those that do have savings, the median working-age family has only $5,000.[4] When it comes to having money for emergencies, it gets worse. In a 2015 Federal Reserve Board report, 47% percent of respondents said they either could not cover an emergency expense costing $400, or they would cover it by selling something or borrowing money.[5]

Without savings, there is no money to invest. As a result, over 40% of Americans do not invest.[6] These Americans are working for money without any of their money working for them. When they stop working, they will have no investments to produce income for them to live on in retirement.

When graduates get jobs that don't cover their student loan, it has significant financial consequences. Student debt has surpassed $1.3 trillion dollars – that's 12 zeros![7] Of that $1.3 trillion, over $66 billion is delinquent, meaning the students are not paying as agreed. Student loan debt is now the largest debt outstanding, excluding real estate mortgages. According to a 2016 American Student Assistance survey, 62 percent of respondents said student debt posed a hardship on their budget when combined with all other household spending. Specifically, 35 percent stated that they found it difficult to buy daily necessities because of their student loans; 52 percent said the debt affected their ability to make larger purchases such as a car, and 55 percent indicated that student loan debt affected their decision or ability to buy a home.[8]

Economic conditions have greatly changed for recent graduates. The job market is now a global market, so competition is beyond just the local demographics. Having a college degree is a good start, but there are other factors that determine a person's Earning Power.

Earning Power is the combination of Knowledge, Experience, Skill, and Character.

> "If you want to have more, you have to become more.
> For things to change, you have to change.
> For things to get better, you have to become better.
> If you improve, everything will improve for you.
> If you grow, your money will grow; your relationships, your health, your business and every external effect will mirror that growth in equal correlation." – Jim Rohn

Maximizing their current Earning Power and constantly increasing it is the most direct way to earn more money. They can increase their earning power by having more specialized knowledge, unique experiences, and soft skills that cannot be easily automated or outsourced. Most important is to have the right character such as humility, determination, a strong work ethic, and gratitude.

Earning more money by increasing one's Earning Power is the best way to save more money. Although there is a limit to how much one can save by reducing expenses, there is no limit to how much one can make by increasing their income.

With medical advancements and healthier lifestyles, people are living longer. Therefore, people need to save more in order to have investments that allow them to retire without outliving their money during retirement. The last thing a retiree wants to do is to be forced to work later in life for money, especially when they could be in poor health. A retiree would much rather live life to the fullest during retirement without worrying about running out of money because they are living longer.

The good news is that they are more ways to generate income in this global economy if you are willing to learn new knowledge and develop new skills.

The key to earning more money is to produce rather than to consume. Being a producer creates economic value by creating solutions to problems. It can be products, services, or a combination of both. The bigger the problem the producer solves the more value he creates so he will naturally earn more money. Since problems can be seen anywhere at any time, opportunities are endless for anyone wishing to make more – just focus on being a problem solver (producer) rather than a consumer.

With the internet and the world connected globally, you can produce value for anyone in any community of any country to earn more money. Even if you have a day job, you can work for a living during the day and work for your financial freedom during the night. As a student, you can study during the day while building your future at night. With computers, the world is "literally" at your fingertips.

Students don't need to wait until they graduate to save and begin investing. With tools and investment resources online, students can practice investing and get into the game earlier. Paper trading allows students to practice analytical skills, determining which companies are smart investments and buying those stocks. Paper trading uses fake money instead of real money, but everything else is the same. If a student has good results that are consistent over time, he may not even need to use his own money to trade. He could have others give him money to invest for them and split the profit. Another alternative is to publish his trades ideas, strategies, and recommendations to paying customers.

If stock investing doesn't sound interesting, a student can practice analyzing real estate investments and put together deals for practice or for sale. It is common for an investor to pay $1,000, $5,000, $10,000, or more depending on the quality of the deal to another investor or a person who can give him a good deal. This works because many investors have the money to invest but don't have the time to do the research and put together deals. When they can make $100,000 on the deal, they will be happy to pay $10,000 for that deal.

As you read this book, you will learn many more ideas and strategies to generate income and make investments. The point I want to make now is that you should get in the game now – don't wait!

Don't let fear cause you to do nothing until you can't do anything. That is how regret happens.

The success of this younger generation of graduates is more important than ever, so fear must not get in the way. While fear is a natural emotion, change the meaning of it from "Forget Everything and Run" to "Face Everything and Rise." (Zig Ziglar)

The generation I am referring to that is so key to our current economy is the Millennials. The U.S. Census Bureau defines Millennials as people born between 1982 and 2000. This is the group that is currently graduating high school up to those in their mid-30s who are professionally working. Currently, the Millennial generation makes up nearly half of the U.S. workforce,[9] and in 2014, Millennials launched almost 160,000 start-ups and made up nearly one-third of all entrepreneurs in the U.S. By 2020, Millennials are expected to account for 30% of retail sales in the United States – that is $1.4 trillion in spending.

However, there is some bad news about our millennial generation.

Millennials earn 20% less than Boomers did at the same stage of life.[10] This can be explained by the fact that they are starting their careers later than the Boomers generation as well as poor economic conditions. New York Times reports that "Millennials are the most educated, worst paid generation." Millennials also have low net worth, down 43 percent from Gen Xers[11] and a 2014 Wells Fargo study found that "45 percent of Millennials are not saving for retirement."

While income may be part of the reason, a more alarming study that tracks college student financial behavior found that college students are less and less responsible with their money than their predecessors.[12] The millennial generation has a higher delinquency rate on their bills than all other age groups. According to a recent study by the American Institute of CPAs, "more than a quarter of millennials surveyed had missed a bill or been contacted by a creditor due to late payments."[13] Experian recently announced that "millennials, as an age group, have the lowest credit scores as well." While some of these characteristics are typical of younger age groups, some are attributed to higher debt.[14] This is bad news, and a financial trend that needs to stop. It's time for a new and better financial direction.

The timing for change has never been more urgent since many are financially illiterate. Only 8% of recent graduates were able to score well when asked to answer basic financial literacy questions.[15] Financial ignorance is a silent crisis. It is a must to have graduates become financially literate and equally important- to be proficient with money skills. The more students and graduates become financially knowledgeable and skilled, the greater their life and the overall economy will be. We must all do our part to help, but ultimately, the students and graduates need to take ownership of their own financial success. Here are my six pieces of advice for them.

1) Take responsibility for your own success.

It's a shame to blame your parents, it's a shame to blame your teachers, and it's a shame to just blame – your success is up to you. It is your responsibility to become better and rise up to challenges. Just remember, if something doesn't challenge you, it won't change you, so embrace it and be grateful for it. You are in control, never forget that.

Take it upon yourself to learn how money works, starting with your everyday life. Don't delay your learning and experiences with money. Start with your family. If you are a student, ask to participate in paying the bills, reviewing financial statements, and join the conversation about money by being an active listener and ask questions.

2) Learn before you go, not as you go.

In the military, as my dad explained to me, if you are surprised, you are dead. Sweat during training so you don't bleed during battle. The more you prepare yourself compared to your competition, the greater the chances will be for your victory. Success is like an iceberg: what is visible on top is only a small fraction of what is below the surface. Success is built upon massive preparation.

Soon you will learn about the Rule of 72 and how time can be the difference between having millions or just thousands of dollars. The earlier you start, and the more skills you develop before you have financial obligations, the more opportunities you will have. The reason why many lose money or don't have money is that they "wing" it. They just do it without any preparation. Making and investing money isn't about taking risk but managing risk. This takes specialized knowledge and skill, and skill takes time and practice. The more you practice, the more skills you will have to work with your money.

3) Get the big picture.

The most e ffective way to get out of a maze is to be able to see it from a bird's eye view – to see the big picture. The money maze is the same. It is complicated to navigate the money maze by going turn by turn. The smart way to get out of the maze and achieve your financial freedom is to have a map that gives you the big picture to see exactly how the paths connect so you can reach your goal and get free. In the next chapters, you will learn exactly how to get the bird's eye view of money with personal financial statements.

4) Learn the language.

Like any subject, there will be vocabulary words specific to it. To know money, you need to know the language to understand it and speak it when asking questions. If you are unable to understand the language, when an opportunity is right in front of you, you will be deaf to it because you don't understand it. When you speak money, you call it to come to you.

5) Know The Connections.

Many financial concepts, strategies, and investments can only be applied when they are understood in relation to one another. With each decision, there will be an opportunity cost associated with it, so the best decisions are made when the opportunity cost is well understood. For example: when is it better to borrow money rather than using your own? Later in this book, you will be able to see how the key financial parts connect to each other to make smart decisions.

6) Practice Money Skills.

Money isn't a concept that can simply be learned without application. Money is a skill that needs development. It needs to be put into practice, to be experienced and learned by action. This book will give you the knowledge, but you will need to put the skills into action to realize their benefits. To help, at the end of the book, I will share with you the money simulation board game that can help you effectively and quickly develop and master your money skills.

The Winning and Losing

As the world continues to interconnect and the economy becomes more intricate, those that are winning and losing become more clear.

Those who are winning:

- Don't sit on the sidelines. They practice money skills and get involved early.
- Are comfortable with numbers and can read financial statements.
- Are aware of current fiscal and economic events so they can stay ahead of their competition.
- Are humble. They admit that they can improve and learn how to increase their employability.
- Increase their earning power by learning new knowledge and developing new skills. They stay valuable by adapting.
- Spend money they have, not borrow from future money to make debt payments
- Spend what is left after savings and not save what's left after spending.

- Practice investing and practice investment analysis with a financial mentor or coach.
- Leverage money taking advantage of good investment deals.

Those who are losing:

- Depend on others for their own financial success and blame others for their mistakes.
- Procrastinate and wait for a better time to start learning and practicing money skills
- Don't keep up with current events or prepare for the changes that are approaching
- Are arrogant, relying on false assumptions and beliefs.
- Are impatient, wanting to enjoy everything now and pay for it later. They spend money they don't have, borrowing against their future ultimately selling themselves short.
- Put savings last on priority to save what's left after spending.
- Don't invest to let their fear cause them to do nothing until they can't do anything.
- Borrow money to spend that basically puts them in a debt prison where they just work to pay off debt with their future paychecks.

The single most effective strategy I have learned and used to build my success was set my ego, pride, and insecurities aside and learn from others who have done it already. What you will learn from this book is not only from my lifetime of knowledge and experience but also those of my mentors and advisors who are not only millionaires but billionaires. I want you to leverage this book to build upon it for your own success. This is why I can't wait to hear what you do with it all!

Chapter Two
MY STORY

"If you are born poor, that's not your mistake. But if you die poor, it is your mistake."-Anonymous

THE ADVERSITY, CHALLENGES, AND STRUGGLES of my parents and family are the foundation of my inspiration to succeed. Knowing what they have been through and what they have done to provide a better life for me, I feel it would be irresponsible and disrespectful not to work hard and become the best that I can be. Settling for less than who I can be is just simply unacceptable and wasteful.

I was born in Vietnam and grew up in a small dirt street down the road from a cemetery. The house I lived in was what most people would consider a shack. The roof was made of palm fronds, the walls were made of hard clay and mud, and the floor was dirt. But to me, that was my home.

My father rose to the rank of Major during the Vietnam War and became a prisoner of war (POW) for over nine years after it ended. In prison, his daily ration of food was just enough to live another day. One day, he counted his food, and it was only 52 corn kernels. Death by malnutrition was commonly combined with the spread of sickness and diseases. Beyond the poor conditions, the psychological torture had prisoners give up on their lives. My father was called many names and ridiculed for being a "loser," but my father swallowed his pride. In response, he would share with them that the responsibilities that were once on his shoulders were now put onto theirs. If the country failed under their leadership, the people would hold the new leadership and not him responsible. My father's strong faith in God and his service-oriented leadership style not only help him survive the POW experience but also made it purposeful.

Over time, my father's health deteriorated, and he began to experience strange illnesses. His heartbeat became irregular and often would skip a beat. He began to fatigue and thought his time to die was coming soon. He prayed. He believed in God's mercy and miracles. He believed that his illnesses would be cured because he didn't deserve them. He lived an honorable life so he believed he wouldn't be left to die like this. He prayed for his fellow brothers in prison. He prayed for how their illnesses could be cured without the need of medicine. He prayed for hope. He prayed for change. He prayed for knowledge.

God did do his miracle, and my father's prayers got answered. My father became aware of a fellow prisoner who owned a book on acupuncture. Acupuncture is an alternative Eastern medical practice that can cure sickness with the use of needles puncturing the human body at key points. My father immediately saw hope in acupuncture because it was curing sickness without the need for medicine. He wanted to learn it and see how he can apply to not only improve his health but also cure the others who are in desperate need of any medical hope.

One of the small monthly luxuries given to each prisoner was a piece of paper they could use to write letters back to their families. To gather enough paper to take notes and document what he learned from the acupuncture book, my dad traded his small ration of corn kernels for the sheets of paper. Till today, he still has those papers. To put into practice, my dad first learned the key points of the body that can help the body heal itself. Instead of needles, he would use heat from wood embers to trigger those points of the body. It worked! He began feeling better, and over time he cured his heart problem.

Further along, he began to use a needle made from a guitar string. He only had one, so he just sterilized it over a burning candle. Day by day, he practiced his skills until he eventually reached the point where he could help his POW brothers.

While my father was in prison, my mother was left alone to care for her four children (which did not include me yet) with no means of support. The children were ages six, four, two, and a recent new born baby. While many suggested she get a divorce, remarry, and put her children up for adoption, her response was always, "If I can give birth to my children, then I can care for them. If they die, I will bury them with my own hands...I am not giving up."

My mother had to figure out how to earn money to survive and feed her children. Initially, she grew fruits and vegetables and then sold them in the street markets. She sold and farmed by day and packaged by night with naps whenever possible. She had to manually seal the produce in plastic bags by holding it over a burning candle. One by one she had to do this. Her efforts brought in enough money to feed the family, but the work was extremely time consuming and earned very little.

One day, while selling her produce in the streets, my mother noticed other people selling fabric. After observing these people for a few days, she thought it would be much less hassle to sell fabric instead of growing fresh produce. She began asking people where she could purchase fabric to sell, but no one would help her because they didn't want more competition. She realized the only way to find the wholesalers was to seek them out herself. After quite a bit of research, she discovered where she could find them. It was far way. It was in another county.

To buy wholesale and then resell at retail, she needed capital. Since she had no money, she had to convince people to lend her money, which was not an easy task and at very high-interest rates. If she didn't pay them back, that would mean danger to her and her family. These debts are personal, so it comes with unimaginable personal methods of collecting a debt. Failure to pay back the debt is not an option.

To go to the next county, she had to travel by bike and carry whatever inventory she bought with her on the bike. Along the way, if she was robbed, that meant she would lose everything. But that's not the main fear. If she can't sell them and turn those fabrics into cash to pay back her debt, that would be a serious problem. Her money loans were all short term.

Thank God, when she begins selling her fabric, on her first day she sold it all. She got the money to pay back what she borrowed and used the profits to reinvest back into more inventory to continue her little business.

During this time, the new government wanted more control of the market, so they were not supportive of entrepreneurial ventures. They had patrol officers who arrested merchants and confiscated everything they had. Any arrest would mean the end of my mother's small business and money. Even worse, being arrested would leave no one to look after her children. Even though my mom had much success running and hiding over the years, her luck ran out one day. She was eventually arrested.

My mother told me she was terrified, and the only thing that helped her was the image of her four children at home and how hard it would be for them to survive without her. My mother knew she had to break free and escape. When she was arrested, she was escorted to headquarters. During the check in, she noticed that the officers were busy doing paperwork and they weren't paying any attention to her. My mother began to side step, inch by inch, towards her stash of inventory and belongings on the confiscation table. Time is running out so, without any chance to hesitate, she quickly snatched her belongings, held them tightly in her arms, and ran out the door without ever looking back.

My mother didn't run home. Instead, she ran to a nearest friend's house and dropped off the stuff so she could run faster. Eventually, she got home to make sure her children were ok. She then took a shower, redressed, and went back to her friend's house. She picked up her things and went right back to selling again. Any day she doesn't sell, there won't be money, so it's back to normal selling while dodging arrests.

To visit my father to bring him food and other necessities, the round trip would take two to three weeks depending on my mother's method of travel (walking, biking, and riding the bus or train, or hitch-hiking) and of course, the weather. The prison was located in the middle of nowhere, far beyond any roads and in the jungle. There was no direct way to get there. Each time my mom visited my dad, she prayed that she would be able to return home safely to take care of the children. Another challenge was that being a woman meant her chances of being robbed, raped, or kidnapped was extremely high, so she had to be very careful and smart about her decisions along this journey. Despite the hardship and challenges, my mom's love for my dad and her unwavering commitment to her family, we all survived. She is our family's hero.

My father lost sight in one eye and hearing in one ear during the war, but he remains spirited throughout his prison sentence. In his later years of prison, he performed what others considered medical miracles with his acupuncture. When he was eventually released and returned home, he continued to help the sick. He put up a "back shack" so there is a place for the sick to come get help. He would on average treat up to sixty patients a day. My dad offered his services for free but asked that those who had the money donate an amount equal to the market price of an egg. A short while later, my brother and I were born. We were one year apart.

Because my father had served in the United States Army and was a POW for more than three years, he and our family qualified for the opportunity to immigrate to America. The year was 1991.

I was five years old. I will never forget my arrival to America and feeling carpet for the first time on the floor mat of my uncle's car driving back from the airport. My feet felt as though they were on clouds. When we arrived at his house, I took off my shoes once again, to experience floor that isn't just dirt. Upon entering the living room, I saw the backyard, and I immediately ran towards it. Bang! That's was when I was formally introduced to glass. I ran directly into the sliding glass door. Everything was new to me, so every new experience was wonderful.

The one new experience that scared me though was going to school. As you already know, I failed kindergarten and only passed it because my brother sat with me.

My journey as an entrepreneur first began when I was twelve years old. I sold candy door to door. The first day I worked twelve hours and only earned ten dollars. Though it was hard work and long hours, I was happy to earn some money. I sold candy for two summers, and that experience taught me a great deal. I learned how to give presentations, handle rejections, and build relationships with customers. But most importantly, I learned the value of hard work and the value of hard earned money.

Around this time, I learned that my parents had been invited by their church to visit Rome. I was very excited for them and could feel their excitement with the opportunity. Then after weeks and months, I didn't see them go anywhere or even hear them mentioning Rome in their conversations. I had to ask them to find out what happened. As it turns out, the trip cost $3,000, and so they declined to go. I asked them if they had the money. They said, "No." Then, after a pause, what they said next hurt me, "even if we had the money, we wouldn't because we need to save money for you."

As you know by now, my parents have had more than their fair share of struggles. I couldn't believe that I was now part of the problem for their life. I feel as if I was the shackles that locked their ankles from living their life. At that moment, I wished I could do something to make money and help them. I couldn't wait until I became 18 years old because I thought that's when I am legally allowed to make money. Until then, I was just a minor, and my signature wasn't valid.

A few years later, I turned 18 years old. It was my last year in high school, and that's when I got the Horatio Alger National Scholar award, and I met my mentor Mark Victor Hansen in Washington D.C.

Within 18 months, I had begun investing and begin building various businesses. Many ended up failing, but the few successes more than made up for the failed attempts. When I earned my first few thousand dollars, I called up my parent's church.

I met with my parents and said, "You guys are going to Rome."

No words can describe to you the feeling I felt when this happened or how my parents responded to it. What I can say is that my parents deserve the best and I love them so much for all that they have done. They are my true heroes, and I am only who I am because of their love, teaching, and role modeling. Till this day, they still talk about that trip to Rome.

During this time right after high school, I was doing everything I could think of to earn money. I accepted an internship at Credit Suisse First Boston analyzing financials of companies for the summer. I read every book available at that time about money, motivation, and success. During my commutes in the car, I was listening to countless audio tapes on personal development. I further studied and became a licensed registered representative for investments and a licensed insurance professional. I would visit families and help them with financial planning, saving money, and investing. Since I was not even old enough to buy alcohol (required age is 21), many adults didn't take my financial advice very seriously. I guess I was just a kid to them. It didn't help that I looked like I was 11 years old either. Regardless, I made sure they were aware and got financially educated before I left our sessions.

It was difficult to juggle going to school, visiting families to help them with financial planning, and analyzing various real estate investment deals to invest in all while making sure I am not failing college to graduate on time. This led me to learn a big lesson.

Although I was making money, I struggled with time. This was when I learned the importance of making money that didn't depend on me working.

It didn't matter *how much* money I could make; it matters more *how* I make it. I had to figure out how I can make money without it always depending on me. This lead me to learn how to build automated income streams, invest in passive income investments, and build businesses that can be operated by other people who I can hire or contract. By the time I graduated college, I had made $4.3 million dollars within my last 24 months of college.

I consider my college years, my golden years to build success. I was told to, "Enjoy your college years as your college years are going to be the best years of your life." That sounded awful to me because if that were true, it would have meant that my life after college was going to be, not so good? I wanted to make sure that my life after college was going to be a great and successful life, so I worked hard during my college years.

As a student, I didn't have the same life responsibilities as a working adult. It was a great time for me to take risks since there was very little, if anything, to lose. I remembered seeing a statistic that read nine out of ten businesses fail. I thought, "Great! All I had to do was to start ten businesses, and one is guaranteed to work!" To me, I realized it was just a matter of time. The earlier I got started, the sooner I could succeed. Failure is inevitable, so I just need to fail quickly and fail forward. Once I got that out of the way, success was what's left for me to have.

My grandfather had a great rule for young people. That rule was that young people had no right to complain about how difficult things are or about being poor. That right to complain was only reserved for the terminally ill and the defenseless elderly. If things got tough, the only choice was to become better. No complaining. Whenever I failed, this rule kept me focused on moving forward.

As I conclude the story here, I want to leave you with my father's words about failing and money. He said, "When you lose money, you've lost nothing. When you lose your self-confidence, you've lost something. But when you quit, you've lost everything."

Chapter Three
MONEY SMARTS OVERVIEW

"Wealth is the product of man's capacity to think."-Ayn Rand

I DEFINE MONEY SMARTS AS having both financial literacy and proficiency. In other words, it's the combination of money knowledge and skills. It takes both to create and sustain wealth.

To give you an overview of Money Smarts, in this chapter you will learn:

1) How money is communicated and recorded, grows and multiplies, and why it matters.
2) The four foundations of money: making money, saving money, investing money, and borrowing money.
3) The 3 big obstacles that prevent people from achieving financial success and how to overcome them.

Money Basics

How Money Is Communicated and Recorded

Whether it is personal or business, information about money is communicated formally using statements or reports called "financial statements" or simply "financials." Business owners or managers base their decisions on the numbers in the financial statements. If they can't read the statements or understand what the numbers mean, they struggle to make the best decision for the company. Worse, if they can't create financial statements to project their cash needs, they will not have enough cash to support the business and may fail before they have enough time to succeed.

Financially successful people review their financials to make smart decisions, just like any business would do. However, most people can't even create personal financial statements that show what they have and what they need for the future. Even those who can create these statements may be too lazy to do so, believing they can simply keep mental, financial statements based on assumptions. In the old days, it was possible, but it is nearly impossible to do so today with money scattered across multiple bank accounts, savings accounts, retirement accounts, investment accounts, credit accounts, and various payable accounts – not to mention how money is now held in the forms of prepaid cards, gift cards, store credit, and online shopping accounts like PayPal and Amazon. For example, people had $1.2 billion loaded onto Starbucks cards and in the Starbucks mobile app as of the first quarter of 2016.[16]

Reading and creating financial statements is the money equivalent of knowing how to read. Understanding financial statements is a key factor in determining how much to pay in taxes, whether or not a business is a good investment, or whether to take out a loan.

Understanding financial statements is actually quite simple. There are only two pieces: the income statement and the balance sheet.

The income statement shows income and expenses to calculate if the entity (or person) is making money or losing money. It simply adds up total income and subtracts total expenses to determine the profit or loss amount (for business) or net savings or net burn (for a person).

The balance sheet shows assets and liabilities. It simply adds up the total assets and subtracts total liabilities to give the owner's equity (for business) or net worth (for a person). Asset is defined as an item of value owned, such as a car, house, or electronic item.

Liability is defined as a financial obligation or debt, such as a student loan, unpaid credit card balance, car loan, or any other borrowed money.

Here is an example of a financial statement that includes both an income statement and a balance sheet.

Income Statement	
Income	**Expense**
1. Income A-$100	1. Expense A-$40
2. Income B-$100	2. Expense 2-$40
3.`Income C-$100	3. Expense 3-$40
Total Income: **$300**	Total Expense: **$120**
Company: Net Profit/Net Loss (Total Income-Total Expense) **Net Profit: $180** [$300-$120]	
Individual: Net Savings/Net Burn (Total Income-Total Expense) **Net Savings: $180** [$300-$120]	

Balance Sheet	
Assets	**Liability**
1. Asset A-$2,000	1. Debt 1-$1,000
2. Asset B-$2,000	2. Debt 2-$1,000
3.`Asset C-$2,000	3. Debt 3-$1,000
Total Asset: **$6,000**	Total Liability: **$3,000**
Company: Owner's Equity (Total Asset-Total Liability) **Owner's Equity: $3,000** [$6,000-$3,000]	
Individual: Net Worth (Total Asset-Total Liability) **Net Worth: $3,000** [$6,000-$3,000]	

Let's take a closer look at each, starting with reviewing the income statement.

Income Statement		
Income	**Expense (lower than income)**	**Expense (higher than income)**
1. Income A-$100	1. Expense A-$40	1. Expense A-$100
2. Income B-$100	2. Expense 2-$40	2. Expense 2-$110
3.`Income C-$100	3. Expense 3-$40	3. Expense 3-$120
Total Income: **$300**	Total Expense: **$120**	Total Expense: **$330**
Company: Net Profit /Net Loss (Total Income-Total Expense)	**Net Profit:** **$180** [$300-$120]	**Net Loss:** **($30)** [$300-$330]
Individual:Net Savings /Net Burn (Total Income-Total Expense)	**Net Savings:** **$180** [$300-$120]	**Net Burn:** **($30)** [$300-$330]

In the above personal income statement, focus first on the key numbers:

- Total Income: $300
- Total Expense: $120 or $330
- Net Savings: $180 or Net Burn: ($30)

Note: Parentheses are often used around the number to show that it is a negative number in financial statements.

Depending if the expense is lower or higher than income, the person will either have a Net Savings or a Net Burn amount. Net Burn means the person is "burning money" by spending more money than they make. I use the term "burn" because you are burning a hole in your savings or checking account to cover the overspending. For example, if there is money in a savings account, the savings will be "burned" up using it to pay for expenses that the amount of income was not enough to cover.

Next, let's review the Balance Sheet more closely.

Balance Sheet		
Assets	**Liability (lower than assets)**	**Liability (higher than assets)**
1. Asset A-$2,000	1. Debt 1-$1,000	1. Debt 1-$2,100
2. Asset B-$2,000	2. Debt 2-$1,000	2. Debt 2-$2,200
3. Asset C-$2,000	3. Debt 3-$1,000	3. Debt 3-$2,300
Total Asset: **$6,000**	Total Liability: **$3,000**	Total Liability: **$3,600**
Company: Owner's Equity (Total Asset-Total Liability)	**Owner's Equity: $3,000** [$6,000-$3,000]	**Owner's Equity: ($600)** [$6,000-$6,600]
Individual: Net Worth (Total Asset-Total Liability)	**Net Worth: $3,000** [$6,000-$3,000]	**Net Worth: ($600)** [$6,000-$6,600]

In the above personal balance statement, focus first on the key numbers:

- Total Asset: $6,000
- Total Liability: $3,000 or $3,600
- Net Worth: $3,000 or ($600)

Depending if the Liability is lower or higher than the Asset, the person will either have a positive or negative Net Worth. When a person has a negative Net Worth amount, that means that person owes more than he owns.

How does a person get in a position to have a negative net worth with more money owed than owned?

Meet Joe

Joe just turned 18 years old and recently graduated high school. On his free time, he likes to fix things like bicycles, electronics, and cars. He currently has no money and needs a car to get a job. His assets only included his personal items. This is Joe's current Personal Balance Sheet

Balance Sheet	
Assets	**Liability**
1. Cash-$0	
2. Lifestyle Asset-Personal Items $1,000 (computer, clothing, and other items Joe owns)	
Total Asset: **$1,000**	Total Liability: **$0**
Individual: Net Worth (Total Asset-Total Liability) **Net Worth: $1,000)** [$1,000-$0]	

Joe didn't think too much and went to a car dealership and buys a brand new car. He gets an auto loan that doesn't need any cash up front because Joe has no cash. See Joe's updated Balance Sheet:

Balance Sheet	
Assets	**Liability**
1. Cash-$0	*1. Brand New Car Loan $15,000*
2. Lifestyle Asset-Personal Items $1,000 (computer, clothing, and other items Joe owns)	
3. Lifestyle Asset-Brand New Car $13,500 ($1,500 depreciation)	
Total Asset: **$14,500**	Total Liability: **$15,000**
Individual: Net Worth (Total Asset-Total Liability) **NEGATIVE Net Worth: ($500)** [$14,500-$15,000]	

Notice in this balance sheet, Joe bought a new car and financed it with no down payment.

The car is an asset (remember, an asset is an item of value owned), so the value of the car is listed on the asset side of the balance sheet. The car loan is a liability (remember, a liability is a financial obligation or debt). Logically, the value of the car will equal the value of the car loan, and the balance sheet will be even (or balanced). However, once a person buys a brand new car and drives it, can he resell that car for the same price he paid for it? No, he will have to sell it for less because its value has depreciated.

Think of anything else a student might buy that depreciates-upon buying it, if the student were to sell it; it would be for a lesser amount than the purchase price. Electronic devices are a common example of items that depreciate.

So to accurately communicate what's happening in this balance sheet, the car asset has depreciated below the car loan amount, which caused Joe to have a negative net worth.

On the other hand, the term to describe an asset increasing in value is appreciation.

Joe quickly realizes he needs to do something to make himself financially better. He reviewed his Earning Power (knowledge, experience, skill, and character) and decided he will maximize his knowledge and skill of fixing cars to turn his balance sheet around.

Joe found a used broken car that he knows he can easily fix. From his experience, he knows that after he fixes the car, the car will appreciate in value. Since Joe doesn't have any cash, he also financed it without any cash with another auto loan.

Balance Sheet	
Assets	**Liability**
1. Cash-$0	1. Brand New Car Loan $15,000
2. Lifestyle Asset-Personal Items $1,000 (computer, clothing, and other items Joe owns)	2. *Broken Used Car Loan: $2,000*
3. Lifestyle Asset-Brand New Car $13,500 ($1,500 depreciation)	
4. *Investment-Value After Broken Used Car Repaired: $5,000 ($3,000 appreciation)*	
Total Asset: **$19,500**	Total Liability: **$17,000**
Individual: Net Worth (Total Asset-Total Liability) **Net Worth: $2,500** [$19,500-$17,000]	

Notice in this balance sheet, Joe's net worth is now positive. He bought the used car for $2,000 with an auto loan, and he fixed it. After it was fixed, the value of the car increased by $3,000. Before he had a negative net worth of $500; now he has a positive net worth of $2,500.

While having a positive net worth is on the right path to financial success, it is important to understand the distinction between net worth and liquid net worth. The problem is that Joe still has no cash.

Liquid net worth is money and assets that you can easily use. For example, although your car is an asset and it has monetary value, you cannot quickly "liquidate" it into cash to buy food or to invest. It is not reasonable to liquidate any lifestyle assets such as a car, clothes, shoes, or home to buy everyday things. Thus, assets purchased to support a lifestyle are not part of the liquid net worth calculation.

Currently, Joe has two cars. If he uses his second car that he fixed as a weekend fun car, he cannot count it as part of his liquid net worth. On the other hand, if he sells the repaired car to realize the profits from the appreciation, he can have the cash. The cash amount will be part of his liquid net worth. See Joe's updated balance sheet when he sells the repaired car.

Balance Sheet	
Assets	**Liability**
1. Cash-$3,000 ($5,000 Sold Car-$2,000 To Pay Off Loan)	1. Brand New Car Loan $15,000
2. Lifestyle Asset-Personal Items $1,000 (computer, clothing, and other items Joe owns)	*2. Broken Used Car Loan: $2,000*
3. Lifestyle Asset-Brand New Car $13,500 ($1,500 depreciation)	
4. Investment-Value After Broken Used Car Repaired: $5,000 ($3,000 appreciation)	
Total Asset: **$17,500**	Total Liability: **$15,000**
Individual: Net Worth (Total Asset-Total Liability) **Net Worth: $2,500** [$17,500-$15,000]	
Individual: Liquid Net Worth (Total Net Worth-Non-Liquid Asset) **Liquid Net Worth: $1,500** [$2,500-$1,000]	

As you can now see, this is one quick example of how Joe used his Money Smarts to create value from his earning power and turn that value into cash by understanding asset appreciation. This is the fundamental business model for businesses that buy and sell used cars. It is also the model for "flipping houses" in real estate, or buying ugly houses in need of repair and fixing and prettying them up to sell for profit.

Let's Review

The income statement shows total income and total expense. When income is higher than expense, the statement shows Net Savings. On the other hand, if the expense is higher than income, the statement shows Net Burn. This Net Savings or Net Burn carries over to the balance sheet in the cash amount. Here is the picture to show the relationship between the income statement and balance sheet. The Net Savings amount is added to the Cash Account in the Balance Sheet. If the savings are negative to have a "net burn" amount, the cash in the balance sheet will be reduced ("burned").

Income Statement	
Income	**Expense**
1. Income A-$100	1. Expense A-$60
2. Income B-$200	2. Expense 2-$60
Total Income: **$300**	Total Expense: **$120**
Individual: Net Savings/Net Burn (Total Income-Total Expense) **Net Savings: $180** [$300-$120]	
Balance Sheet	
Assets	**Liability**
1. CASH (+Net Savings $180 from income)	
Total Asset: **$180**	Total Liability: **$0**
Individual: Net Worth (Total Asset-Total Liability) **Net Worth: $180** [$180-$0]	

To review the concept of the Balance Sheet, a Balance Sheet calculates the Net Worth number by taking the total assets and subtracting the total liabilities. When the assets have more value than the liabilities, net worth is positive. When liabilities are higher than assets, net worth is negative.

Remember that liquid net worth doesn't include lifestyle assets, as those assets are for personal use and not available to sell for cash. Only assets that can be quickly liquidated are included in the liquid net worth calculation.

By now, you can see how a financial statement that includes both income statement and balance sheet gives you a clear overall financial picture of a person or business. In the coming chapters, I will go further into detail. For now, I will discuss how money grows. Once you learn how money grows, you will see the why it is important to have savings to build up your investment capital. Capital is the term to describe the money you save for investments.

How Money Grows & Multiplies

I have a decision for you to make. Which one of the following of two Christmas gift options would you like to receive from me?

Gift Option A: Receive $1 million dollars cash today

Gift Option B: Receive an account that has 1 penny today but whose value doubles every day for the month of December (31 days). For instance, tomorrow, you have two pennies. It grows to four pennies the day after tomorrow

If you are unsure, still make a decision. Making a decision is better than not making one. In actuality, making no decision in this scenario is like choosing option C, which is nothing, and then regretting not at least have given it a try. Don't bench yourself. It's ok to be wrong and fail, but the only way to win is to be in the game, giving you the chance to win.

So, make a decision.

Let's now fast forward twenty days. If you chose Option A, congratulations so far because, after day 20, Option B is only worth $5,242.88. One million dollars is a lot more than that. Those of you who chose Option B, are you having second thoughts? Do you want to change your decision? If so, you can do so now.

Let's move forward five more days. If you switched from B to A, congratulations. Thus far, after 25 days, Option B is still only worth $167,772.16. Compared to Option A of one million dollars, Option A is so far the better choice. For those who stuck with Option B, do you want to change your mind now? This is the last chance you get to switch to Option A.

Let's move to the end of the month, December 31, if you chose Option A at the beginning, or switched during the month from B to A, congratulations on getting your one million dollars. Those who chose Option B and didn't change their mind, today your account is valued at over $10 million dollars ($10,737,418.24, to be exact). Congratulations to those who chose Option B and were patient enough to watch their money grow and multiply.

Building wealth is not all about timing the market, going in and out with short term trades, but about letting it grow over the long-term and leveraging the power of "compound interest."

Compound Interest is defined by Merriam-Webster dictionary as "interest computed on the sum of an original principal and accrued interest." To understand that definition, you will need to understand the term "principal." Principal is the money that is invested or lent. To best understand it is to see it in action, so here is the full 31 days of "compound interest" at work with the principal amount of 1 penny (Option B from the above example):

Day 1: $0.01
Day 2: $0.02
Day 3: $0.04
Day 4: $0.08
Day 5: $0.16
Day 6: $0.32
Day 7: $0.64
Day 8: $1.28
Day 9: $2.56
Day 10: $5.12
Day 11: $10.24
Day 12: $20.48
Day 13: $40.96
Day 14: $81.92
Day 15: $163.84
Day 16: $327.68
Day 17: $655.36
Day 18: $1,310.72
Day 19: $2,621.44
Day 20: $5,242.88
Day 21: $10,485.76

Day 22: $20,971.52
Day 23: $41,943.04
Day 24: $83,886.08
Day 25: $167,772.16
Day 26: $335,544.32
Day 27: $671,088.64
Day 28: $1,342,177.28
Day 29: $2,684,354.56
Day 30: $5,368,709.12
Day 31: $10,737,418.24

Amazing how a single penny of principal can earn $10,737,418.23 of interest in 31 days with the power of compound interest.

Compound interest has the power to make you rich, but it also has the power to make you a money slave. Just imagine that the above account is not your savings account where your money is growing but a credit card account where your debt is growing. When borrowing money, the penny is your principal debt amount. Remember, the term principal is both money invested and money borrowed.

For example, you purchased a computer for $2,500 using a credit card that charged 30% interest. The credit card only required you to pay the minimum due amount of $75 the first month. Excited to see the low monthly payment, you kept paying the minimum $75 amount per month using auto pay. At this rate, it took you six years (72 months) of paying $75 per month to pay off the computer, and the total amount you paid the credit card company was $5,400. I am sure you did a lot of research to get the lowest price, comparing different shops and searching for coupons and discounts, but all that effort was washed away by paying the minimum credit card payments and allowing compound interest to work against you. This is how compound interest can turn you into a money slave as you work just to pay off the interest, barely touching the principal.

Knowing how to calculate compound interest is foundational for your Money Smarts. Estimating compound interest can be quick and simple if you know the "Rule of 72."

Rule of 72

The Rule of 72 is a shortcut to estimating the number of years required to double your money at a given annual rate of return. The rule states that you divide the rate, expressed as a percentage, into 72.[17]

72 ÷ compound annual interest rate = years required to double investment

It is important to remember to use the rate as a whole number, not a decimal when using this formula. If the compound annual interest rate is 12%, the number used to enter into this formula is "12" rather than "0.12" (or 12% expressed as a decimal).

Using the formula, we see that investments with a 12% compound annual interest rate double in approximately six years.

72 ÷ 12 = 6 years

For a balance on a credit card with a 30% interest charge, assuming no monthly payments are being made toward the principal, this formula shows how quickly the debt balance doubles:

72 ÷ 30 = 2.4 years (2 years, 5 months)

At a glance, you can see how quickly your debt, the money you owe, can grow faster than your investments. Earning 12% with an investment is considered a high rate of return, but it is low compared to the 30% credit card interest rate. This is one of the reasons why people struggle financially and have negative net worth when calculating their balance sheet. Psychologically, the reason why many don't want to do their balance sheet is that it is not what they want to see. Being Money Smart begins with being honest with yourself and understanding where you are at now so you can plan where you want to be. Without a starting line, it is not possible to make progress towards your goal and cross the finish line. This leads to my last point in this "understanding money" section.

How Money Matters Throughout A Lifetime

At some point in life, almost everyone is forced to stop working. At such time, one does not want to worry about money. The term for this period is "retirement."

I define retirement as the time during which you work because *you want to*, not because *you have to* to earn money.

For me, achieving retirement when I am young is achieving "true retirement." Achieving retirement will not be great if the retiree doesn't have the health to enjoy the retirement. True retirement means that retirees can enjoy it. Certainly, this involves taking care of their health while young, being sure not to neglect it while working hard to earn money. Since health reduces as people age, the earlier a retiree achieves true retirement, the more time, energy, and health remain to enjoy it. It is never easy to think about death. But to know that our time is limited is important. It gives us a sense of urgency to not let precious time go by without giving our best efforts to live to the fullest.

To help me understand the value of time and to motivate myself to work hard, I made a simple life timeline and wrote what my life focus would be at different age ranges. This is personal to me, so everyone will be different, but here is my example.

Age	Health Level	Focus
0-5	A	Learning life's fundamentals
5-18	A	Going to school to get fundamental education
19-22	A	Professional and career preparation
23-30	A	Dedication to work
30-50	B	Dedication to family while working
50-67	C	Maximizing life
68-100+	D	Celebrating life

When I look at this timeline, it is very clear that I don't have much time. Especially when looking at the health level, I don't have many years of level A and B health available. It would be ideal to achieve true retirement, or financial retirement, as early as possible to have the best health. The current retirement age is 67 years old, so that gives me roughly 47 years to work for my money. However, looking closely at the 47 years, only about ten years can be fully dedicated to working; the other years have many other life responsibilities that can be more important to be dedicated to, such as family. In some ways, this is why there isn't enough time to work. This is why having monthly net savings is very important when a person is young because as life responsibilities increase, so do the expenses, which lower the monthly net savings.

Considering the time factor, the earlier a person starts learning about money and developing money skills, the more time he has to accumulate, invest, and grow wealth to achieve financial retirement as soon as possible. Again, financial retirement doesn't mean the retiree does not work at all. It means the retiree does not HAVE TO work for money, so he has the time to do whatever he finds to fulfill him. Furthermore, the retiree can do things that can change the world for greater. If it so happens that the work he does that fulfills him in retirement is the same work that made him the money to retire, then he chooses to continue working because he WANTS TO, not because he needs to.

The Four Foundational Skills of Money

The four foundational skills of money are the four sections that make up the financial statements: Income, Expenses, Assets, and Liabilities. The Income section is about making money, the Expense section is about saving money, the Asset section is about investing money, and the Liability section is about borrowing and leveraging money. This section gives a brief overview of each, and the following chapters go into detail and provide strategies for each of the four foundational skills.

Income: Making Money

The ways to make money are endless with a creative mind. However, to help guide your understanding and give you a foundation, I have grouped the ways of making money into four income groups: Time-based, Performance-based, Investment-based, and Benefit-based. Certainly, there are hybrids which combine two or more types of income, but these four categories cover the vast majority of incomes to give you a solid foundation of potential income that you can create for yourself.

Time-based Income depends on the person actively working to produce the income. As a result, income is paid based on the worker's time. Within the time-based income group, there are two ways to get paid, hourly or salary.

Hourly: These are jobs that pay per hour. Governments do set a minimum hourly wage that companies must pay these workers to prevent unfair wages. As a benchmark, people work full time if they work eight hours per day from Monday to Friday, which totals forty hours per week. Anyone working less is considered part-time, where the hours are closer to 20 hours a week. This standard is important because overtime laws require companies to pay their workers more per hour if they are asked to work more than the standard eight hours per day or forty hours per week. Usually, the overtime pay is 1.5 times higher than normal hourly rate. For example, if a person normally gets paid $10 per hour, but works overtime, then that person will get paid $15 for each hour of overtime.

Salary: These are jobs that do have their workers work full time, but that are not paid by the hour. A salaried worker may work less or more than the standard forty hours per week but are paid a fixed amount per paycheck. Salaried workers often find themselves working much more than forty hours a week, but their pay can also be much higher than hourly work even though they are not getting paid overtime.

Performance-based Income depends on the person's time and performance to produce the income. The person may spend a whole day working and make zero money. Because of this income risk, most people negotiate a time-based income such as an hourly or salary to provide a base level of income, with additional performance-based income, usually commission or a bonus. With this combination, the worker has a minimum payment amount that they can expect to live on during times of low performance. In situations where the commission opportunity is high enough that no base is needed, as long as the person is performing well, they make enough income. The potential for commission-only pay may allow a person to spend only one hour per day working but make more than the average person makes in a week.

Contract pay as an independent contractor is another type of performance pay in which the income is pre-negotiated, or contracted, with an agreed amount. Based on reputation and past performance, a contractor can set higher amounts. The more knowledge, skill, experience, and overall value the contractor can demonstrate, the more he can ask for in compensation. For example, movie actors may have low starting contracts, but once they demonstrate great performance in their initial movies, they can negotiate higher-paying contracts for future movies.

Profit draws and profit sharing are other types of performance pay, in which income is based on the performance of the business. Business owners or partners can earn high or low income. It is all dependent on their leadership and management skills.

Investment-based Income does not depend on the person's time working but rather produces income from investments with little to no personal involvement. Examples include real estate rental income, portfolio income, and businesses in which the owner is not actively involved. Investment income is key to financial freedom and achieving true retirement.

Benefit-based Income comes from family, government, and other external sources. For example, if students don't work while going to school, they still might receive benefit income in the form of having their expenses paid for. Just because the students don't pay for their living expenses such as food, water, and shelter, doesn't mean they don't have expenses. They do have those expenses, and those expenses are paid by the benefit income they get from their families. Other examples include welfare, grants, financial aid, and scholarships.

Expense: Saving Money

Just like ways to earn money, ways to spend money are also endless with a creative mind. This is why it is important for each individual to develop strategies that best fit their own values, character, and personality. It doesn't matter which strategy each person chooses or how unique it is; it just matters that he develops or finds one that gives him the desired result of spending less and saving more. This is why it is not effective for me to give you any definite ways. Rather, I hope to give you the foundation to help you develop your own most effective way. To begin guiding you, I have grouped the ways of spending money into three types of expenses, Fixed Expenses, Variable Expenses, and Discretionary Expenses.

Fixed Expenses occur monthly at the same amount. Examples of these expenses are housing payments, car payments, student loan payments, and cell phone payments. These fixed expenses usually have a pre-set, agreed upon amount, so these expenses must be renegotiated with the recipient to reduce or eliminate them. Many people believe that negotiation is impossible or too hard, but it might surprise them just how powerful asking is when it is done in a sincere and authentic way (and with a little persistence, in some cases).

Variable Expenses occur monthly but at different amounts. Examples of this expense are utilities, groceries, child care, pet care, and variable loan payments. These expenses are often necessities similar to fixed expenses, but they differ in that the payer can directly control how much or how little per month is spent, at least to some degree. For example, a payer may find ways around the house to save electricity or buy groceries at discount supermarkets to save money.

The biggest expense here to be cautious of is the variable loan payment. Remember the earlier example of using a credit card to purchase a $2,500 computer, ultimately paying $5,400 by making only the minimum payment for six years? Credit card companies suggest that you make these easy minimum payments, usually 3% of the balance, so they can make money. This is why for the first month, the credit card company only requires $75 on a $2,500 purchase, as the $75 represents 3% of the $2500 debt balance. In the example, I set the monthly payment to $75 per month. The dangerous reality is, the credit card company adjusts the minimum payment due each month based on the outstanding debt balance. If the borrower sets their credit card repayment to auto pay the minimum monthly payments, or 3% of the balance, the monthly minimum payments go down over time just like the outstanding principal does. Here is the math for the first twelve months of payments:

Month	Minimum Payment Due (3%)	Interest Payment (30%)	Principal Payment	Balance
1	$75.00	$62.50	$12.50	$2,487.50
2	$74.63	$62.19	$12.44	$2,475.06
3	$74.25	$61.88	$12.38	$2,462.69
4	$73.88	$61.57	$12.31	$2,450.37
5	$73.51	$61.26	$12.25	$2,438.12
6	$73.14	$60.95	$12.19	$2,425.93
7	$72.78	$60.65	$12.13	$2,413.80
8	$72.41	$60.35	$12.07	$2,401.73
9	$72.05	$60.04	$12.01	$2,389.72
10	$71.69	$59.74	$11.95	$2,377.78
11	$71.33	$59.44	$11.89	$2,365.89
12	$70.98	$59.15	$11.83	$2,354.06

The table shows that the first $75 payment only reduced the outstanding balance from $2,500 to $2,487.50 because $62.50 of that $75 went to the credit card interest (their profit). Only $12.50 of the $75 goes to pay down the principal debt balance. The table also shows how the minimum amount due goes down as the principal goes down. The first payment is $75, but then it drops to $74.63 for the second, and down to $70.98 on the twelfth payment. Because the credit card is set to auto-pay the minimum due, it is a "variable loan payment." While it feels good to the borrower to pay less and less per month, this is dangerous and costly. The $2,500 in this scenario ultimately costs $13,725.65 and takes 40 years to pay off! The credit card company earns a profit of $11,225.65 from interest. This is why I am making a strong effort to discuss this "variable loan payment" and giving you a big warning NOT TO DO IT. Do not set up payments for your credit card or any loan account to the minimum amount due.

Minimum payments can disqualify you from getting the 0% interest promotion. Usually, 0% interest credit card promotions require the balance to be paid off within a certain number of months. When you do not pay it off by their set promo date, not only will you begin to pay high interest on the debt balance but also you will need to pay the backdated interest. Even if you set auto payments that "should" pay the promo credit card off by the deadline, it is best to confirm and check because mistakes can and will happen. For any reason that you missed the deadline and see your debt balance increased by the large backdated interest, call them immediately. They should be able to help you, but there might be a small window of opportunity that they can help so don't wait to call.

Discretionary Expenses occur at varying times from month to month and at a varying amount. Some examples of these expenses are shopping, dining out at restaurants, and entertainment. These expenses are usually "wants" and not "needs," but the meaning can be defined differently for each person. Many of the fixed and variable expenses are loan payments of purchases that can be "wants" too, such as an expensive computer or luxury car. The key point to understand for these discretionary expenses is that it is up to the spender. It is at the spender's "discretion," and he should make the best decision possible to maximize his net monthly savings. To help you frame your mind to spend less, think about wealth being measured on how little one needs rather than how much one has.

Assets: Investing Money

Investing is the key vehicle to build wealth and become rich. Many are confused about this and believe that the way to becoming rich is to have a high paying career and job. While it certainly helps to have a high paying job to increase your total income, the only number that matters is the Net Savings amount, which depends on how much of the income is saved after subtracting monthly expenses. It is not uncommon for people who have high paying jobs to have expensive lifestyles and little to no monthly Net Savings. One-third of high-income earners don't save at all and are living paycheck to paycheck.[18] The key is the monthly Net Savings amount from the personal income statement. My goal is to convince you to save 50% of your income. To do so, you could spend 50% of your current income, or you could double your income while keeping your current total expenses the same. Remember that your Net Savings amount is the cash that you can use as capital to invest. The more capital you have, the more opportunities you have to invest. The more investments you have, the quicker you can have your investment produce so you can achieve true retirement. Many people who earn high time-based income but don't invest believe their time is money. Thus, they wish for more time so they can make more money. It is really sad because they won't achieve this. It's not possible for them to make more money because nobody can have more time than the twenty-four hours in a day. Investments are the key to increase money without depending on time.

There are two ways in which investments create money for the investor, through income and capital gains.

Income Investments are investments that can provide income for you in which income doesn't depend on your time or your performance. The term used to describe these investments is "passive income" investments. Examples of income producing investments are real estate rentals and stocks that pay out regular dividends. The goal is to have your investments produce enough income to retire, but how much is that, exactly? A handy rule of thumb is that total income producing investments need to be worth approximately 25 years of expenses and generate at least 4% income.

See the math:

Approximately, how much money can allow you to retire?
Answer: 25 years of expenses.

Monthly expense: $5,000 (annual total: $60,000)
25 Years' worth of expense: $60,000 x 25 = $1,500,000
Total Income Producing Investments: $1,500,000
Minimum Investment Income of 4% per year: $1,500,000 x 0.04 = $60,000

As the above math illustrates, the income produced by the investment covers the annual expense amount of $60,000 a year. What this means is that your investment income allows you to retire such that you no longer have to work to pay your expenses but only work if you want to. Certainly, there are many other factors to consider, such as expenses increasing, earning greater or less than 4% on investments, and taxes that can change the math. The key point is that you now know the approximate amount needed to achieve your retirement goal and that it really depends on how much your lifestyle expenses you set to be. The more you can increase your monthly Net Savings amount and use capital gains to build up your investment fund, the sooner you can achieve your financial freedom.

Capital Gain Investments are investments which can appreciate in value for you to sell for gains. Instead of holding onto the asset, you can sell it at the higher price. The profit, or gain, from the sale of the asset, is the "capital gain." What makes capital gains powerful is that they increase the cash available to invest in new assets. The more assets an investor buys and owns, the more income and capital gains can be earned. This is how your money grows and works for you. Assets can also protect against inflation. While inflation increases cost, it can also drive appreciation of assets, so the invested money will not decay in value. The only money that can decay is cash. Money invested into appreciating assets can even produce capital gains totaling more than the monthly net savings number. For example, Chad invested in a house that he bought for $200,000 and rents out for $1,000 a month. However, since he didn't have $200,000 cash to buy that house, Chad borrowed money from a bank through a mortgage loan, with a monthly payment of $1,000 over thirty years. In this example, what Chad pays per month to the bank and what he collects from his renters is the same – $1,000 – so he makes no income on a monthly basis. Of course, this example assumes Chad has no other expenses on the house other than the bank payment. His investment strategy for buying this house was not to produce income but capital gains. Thus, in 5 years, this house is now worth $400,000 because that city is attracting many people who want to live there. The time has come to realize his capital gains, so Chad sells it for $400,000. He earned a $200,000 capital gain in 5 years. That is equivalent to saving $40,000 of cash every year without any hard work compared to having a time-based income.

Liabilities: Borrowing and Leveraging Money

The words liability and debt are usually not the favorite words of many people, but those people cannot be more wrong. Debt can be a great tool to build wealth. When people hear or read about debt, they don't associate it with good feelings or thoughts. For certain people, debt is a bad word or something to be ashamed of, and this negative association is anchored by stories of how debt has ruined people's lives. But, like everything, there are good and bad sides to it. While debt is bad for some people, it can be equally as good for others. Here is a way to distinguish bad debt from good debt.

The difference between good and bad debt is bad debt forces you to work for it while good debt works for you.

Debtors know deep inside which debts are bad when they don't have the money to buy what they want and need to borrow money to buy it. This is the big reason why people end up living paycheck to paycheck. When a debtor borrows money to spend on things, he is spending future income – he basically spent the future paycheck before he even received it. If for some reason, the debtor loses that future income he already spent, he gets into a deeper financial problem as he needs to borrow again. The more a debtor borrows to spend, the more of future income disappears, making it impossible to save and build up any capital funds to invest at all.

Good debt works for the debtor, so he doesn't have to work to pay it off. An example is borrowing money to buy an asset that the borrower can rent out and later sell for profit, such as Chad's house that produced $200,000 in capital gains. On a smaller scale, a debtor can borrow to buy bikes, clothes, or tools to rent. Or a borrower can use debt to buy equipment to manufacture products that can be sold. It can be as simple as buying a printer that prints design work or a computer to use for software development. This is good debt as long as the borrowed money is not spent but invested into owning an asset that can earn.

Banks understand good debt very well, and they love to issue as much of this type of debt as they can find. When a borrower sees a bank, he sees them as a money lender. But in reality, they are big borrowers as well. Where do banks get the money to lend to borrowers? They borrow it from other people, members of the general public who have savings account with them. The bank gives the savings account holder 1% interest each year for keeping money in the savings account and then uses that money to lend to other people at 5%. The bank earns the 4% difference between the two rates as profit. The more banks can borrow from people, the more they can lend. A bank's main business is to create as much good debt as possible.

Biggest Obstacles

By now, you should have a basic idea of how money works and how to earn and invest money. However, you might notice that there are some big obstacles that might prevent you from applying these ideas and getting results for yourself. So I want to share with you three potential obstacles and ideas on how to overcome them.

First, you probably feel that you do not have enough information. To succeed, you need more details and strategies. I will have them in the next four chapters, with each chapter dedicated to one of the four skills that I discussed above.

Second, the most common obstacle to any success is belief, so I want to let you know that the secret of success is that it is 90% belief and 10% effort, but you need to give 100% to reach success. As you may have concluded from my story that I shared in chapter 3, a lot of my growth journey has been mental. When I got started, I had to keep reminding myself that "the only limits I have are the limits I set for myself." It made me feel empowered to become what I believed I could become and to achieve what I wanted to achieve. Being the youngest member of my family and wanting to do things differently was not easy, so I understand the feeling of being the pioneer. Just know, you are not alone. I am putting my heart and soul into this book and have created additional resources to help you which I will share at the end of the book. As I have the words hanging on my home library wall: dream, believe and succeed.

Third, the final big obstacle people have that prevents them from achieving their goals is that they fear setting big goals. If they set these bigger goals and miss them, then they might believe they have failed and feel that they are not good enough and may not be loved by others for failing. Well, I want to share with you the wise words of Jim Rohn, who I met. "The ultimate reason for setting goals is to entice you to become the person it takes to achieve them." As you continue to read this book, I will do my best to help you become the person it takes to achieve your goals.

Chapter Four
MAKING MONEY

"Learn to work harder on yourself than you do on your job. If you work hard on your job, you'll make a living. If you work hard on yourself, you can make a fortune."-Jim Rohn

Income Statement		Balance Sheet	
Income	Expense	Assets	Liability
1. Income A	1. Expense A	1. Asset A	1. Debt 1
2. Income B	2. Expense 2	2. Asset B	2. Debt 2
3.`Income C	3. Expense 3	3. Asset C	3. Debt 3
Total Income: **$ABC**	Total Expense: $123	Total Asset: $ABC	Total Liability: $123

Company: Net Profit/Net Loss (Total Income-Total Expense)
Net Profit: $

Company: Owner's Equity (Total Asset-Total Liability)
Owner's Equity: $

Individual: Net Savings/Net Burn (Total Income-Total Expense)
Net Savings: $

Individual: Net Worth (Total Asset-Total Liability)
Net Worth: $

THIS CHAPTER IS ALL ABOUT income. You will learn the #1 secret for making more money, strategies for earning each of the four specific types of the incomes, how income affects your pay and income planning tips for key life events.

If you agree that paying others their worth and getting paid for your worth is fair, then the only way to increase your pay is to increase your worth. To earn more, you first have to become more. All "overnight successes" took years to get there. Anyone looking for shortcuts will just find themselves cut short of their dreams. If you want to make more, then understand that the fundamental #1 secret for making more money is to increase your earning power which is increasing your knowledge, experience, skills, and character.

Increasing Your Earning Power

Increase Earning Power with Knowledge. The greatest treasures are not sunk at the bottom of the sea, buried in the ground, or hidden in secrecy...they are in books waiting for you. Knowledge gives you the ability to understand things that others don't. To gain knowledge, the easiest way is through reading books. The wisdom of the ages has never been more accessible than it is today through books, so anyone who recognizes this treasure can have it. In fact, reading is one of the habits of the ultra-rich, with the richest billionaires reading at least several books a month. Mark Zuckerberg reads a book every two weeks, Bill Gates reads about a book a week, and Warren Buffett reads 500 pages a day.[19]

One common mistake is to replace knowledge with assumption. Opening the door of knowledge requires humility. The seeker must not assume they already have all of the knowledge needed. Growing up, I was told a story of a man who considered himself to be very smart but wanted to gain wisdom from a master. When he met the master, he was offered a cup of tea. As the master poured tea into this man's cup, it overflowed, and yet the master continued to pour until the man yelled, "Stop! The cup is already full!" The master simply replied, "Yes, indeed, and you are just like this cup. How can I teach you anything when you are already full?" From that day forward, I have always made sure that I empty my cup, and I encourage you to do the same.

Increase Earning Power with Skill Experience. "When a man with money meets a man with experience, the man with experience leaves with money, and the man with money leaves with experience."- Anonymous

True knowledge and understanding can only be gained through experience. Experience gives the doer the ability to see things that others won't. Only through experience can a man create his knowledge, built upon the knowledge of others acquired through reading, watching, and listening. For example, riding a bicycle, flying an airplane, and swimming must be experienced as the experiences cannot be shared through words. The greatest knowledge comes from experience.

When you begin to prepare for a career, find a mentor who can offer you experience. Career mentorship will not only help you gain experience in your chosen field but also let you know if it is the career you want to do for the long term. There are many students who borrow money for school, go into debt, and waste years of their life in school only to later find out they hate the career they prepared for. If the student had a career mentor and some hands-on experience, it would have saved money and, more importantly, time.

Developing money skills requires you to experience managing money and making decisions with money. It is important for you to "get into the game" and take personal financial responsibility in your life no matter how young you are. Start with reading your family bills and be involved with paying the bills, even if it is not your money. Get the experience of reading and analyzing a statement as well as the feeling of paying for it. Try using cash to pay for things so you can feel the pain of having money leaving your hands.

Increase Earning Power with Character Development. All the greatest ideas and plans become worthless without the ability to execute them.

A skill is simply the ability to perform what others can't. Ideas can change the world, but without the skills to make things happen, the ideas will simply remain ideas. While many come up with ideas, only a few have the skills to execute them. Skilled individuals have more opportunities than time to take advantage of them all. Skills are not born with people; all skills are developed through practice, with many trial and errors. Yes, it requires error, which means failure, disappointment, and humiliation. Expect it, embrace it, and enjoy it as the more skills you can develop, the better you become and the more opportunities you have. Success is doing what others are not willing to do and being able to handle what others are unable to handle physically, mentally, and emotionally. These skills are what will make you better and more competitive to succeed financially.

In 2017, the Graduate Management Admission Council ® (GMAC), a global nonprofit organization comprised of leading graduate business schools around the world, surveyed a total of 959 employers representing more than 628 companies located in 51 countries worldwide and concluded its finding below:[20]

Relative Importance of Major Skills Sets Employers Require for Mid-Level Jobs:

Rank 1: Communication
Rank 2: Teamwork
Rank 3: Technical
Rank 4: Leadership
Rank 5: Managerial

Higher the ranking means more importance.

Employers ranked communication skills as the most important skill set a mid-level employee could have, followed by teamwork, technical, leadership, and managerial skills. There were some interesting regional variations to note.

The United States and Asia Pacific: Communication and teamwork ranked most important.

Europe: Teamwork ranked most important, followed by communication and technical skills.

Latin America: Leadership, technical skills, and teamwork top-ranked.

To sum this up, the world needs more effective Communicators, with a capital C. That's the number #1 skill in demand globally.

This is not surprising as technology has inhibited students from developing communication skills with more and more students texting, posting on social media, tweeting, and chatting via apps. While these activities can improve written communication, the writing is often informal and can create bad writing habits. Furthermore, most effective Communicators know that much of the message lies not in *what* was said but rather *how* it was said. Nonverbal communication from body language, facial expression, and tonal changes are all important parts of communication that are not being practiced online.

I truly hope this study serves as a wake-up call for students to look up from texting on their mobile devices and start speaking their thoughts using their full body and expressions. The tools that were meant to improve our communication have ultimately made our communication skills worse. The chart above sends a clear message for students, and those who can focus on this key skill and develop as Communicators will certainly out-compete their peers for career opportunities.

Increase Earning Power with Character Development. Character gives you the fortitude to persist when others quit. Character is the foundation of who you are that enables you to become anything you want to be. While credit scores measure how you manage your debt, your WHO Score measures how you manage yourself – your character. Who you are is what attracts, creates, and maintains all your necessary relationships and opportunities for success.

In my opinion, the greatest creature to teach us character is the ants. Here is what we can learn from them:

- **Personal ownership and responsibility.** Ants don't need anyone to hold them accountable; they simply get things done. While ants have a queen, she doesn't give out commands or orders. The ants don't have a boss, manager, or supervisor. Each ant does the task they are specialized in, respects the other ants, and works toward the common goal. The takeaway for students is not to wait until school is over to start being accountable for life. The sooner a student takes responsibility for his life, the earlier he can create and enjoy success. Parents, teachers, and employers will only hold you accountable to a standard. Thus, for you to be above standard and achieve above standard level of success, you need to hold yourself accountable.
- **Perseverance.** Ants would die before they give up. No obstacle or challenge deters the ants. They either go around an obstacle or remove the obstacle. They don't even know what giving up is. The takeaway here is that it is possible never to give up, so don't give up no matter how hard and achieve your goals.
- **Teamwork.** If the work cannot be done by one ant, they will work together to get it done. Teamwork makes the dream work. Learn to work with people because the greatest achievements will often require teams of people.
- **Preparation.** In summer, ants don't simply enjoy the sun; they

begin preparing for the winter. The takeaway here is not to be complacent. To achieve more and get ahead, prepare when others are not. Delay your gratification for longer term fulfillment or survival. Students have the greatest treasure, time, but often waste it. Thus, when the students get older and want more time, they can't have it. Always prepare when you can, especially when you are young and have the energy to do more, accomplish more, and prepare more.

- **Sharing.** Ants share their blessings and gifts with others. When the ants find anything great that can be shared, they bring it back to the hive.

The 2016 Corporate Recruiters Survey asked employers to identify those skills and traits they feel are the most important when evaluating MBA and non-MBA graduates as potential new hires for their companies.[21] Below are the twelve skills and traits they identified:

1) Fit with company culture
2) Ability to work in and build strong teams
3) Ability to make an impact
4) Adaptable
5) Strong business ethics
6) Leadership potential
7) Ability to use data to tell a story
8) Insightful
9) Work independently
10) Curiosity
11) Executive presence
12) Ability to build external networks

Together, knowledge, experience, skill, and character are the four fundamental personal development areas that increase earning power and enable the earner to create all the opportunities needed to succeed in life. Without these personal developments, even if the opportunity is right in front of him, the earner may not recognize it or have the ability to take advantage of it. Opportunities may appear to be determined by luck, but they are created. The more an earner prepares, the "luckier" he seems to be.

Strategies for Creating Income

In this chapter, I have reviewed the four types of income: Time-based Income, Performance-based Income, Investment-based Income, and Benefit-based Income. Now I am going into the details of each income type by providing you with specific strategies to increase your income within each type.

Time-based Income Strategies.

To earn time-based income from a job, the earner will need to be hired for that job. Thus, I will share some strategies for how you the earner can land a great job.

Let's begin with a few points of reference about the hiring process and the job market overall.

Reference Point 1: There are three main steps in the hiring process. The earner's simple goal is to complete all the steps. Thus, if you are not getting to step 2, the interview, work to improve your first step. View this as a funnel through which an employer filters its candidates.

> STEP 1: Application, cover letter, and resume.
> STEP 2: Interview.
> STEP 3: Job offer and acceptance.

Reference Point 2: Reframe your understanding of the "Job Market" as a "Solution-Needs Market." Every job or position is a solution to an organization's problem or need. Seek to understand what the problem or need is and become the solution. When jobs and positions go unfulfilled, it means the employer cannot find the right solution in the applicants and may be forced to look for other ways to solve their problems. This is why there are two common complaints, one from each side of the table. Job seekers complain that there are not enough job opportunities, while employers complain that there are not enough qualified people to fill the jobs they have open.

Reference Point 3: Not all jobs are advertised. Speaking to a company representative might mean that the earner is on an interview without even knowing it. Imagine that you are an employer. If you happen to run across an amazing person with great knowledge, experience, skill, and character, would you consider creating a position for them in your company or find some way to bring that person onto your team? Human capital is always the greatest asset for a company to invest in, and when you as the earner can bring value to others, you will be employable anywhere.

Key Strategies for Getting Hired

1) Show You Are the Right Fit

- Customize every cover letter, application, and resume to each specific potential employer. The application is often the job seeker's first impression, so use it to show the prospective employer that you are a fit. To know whether you are a fit, first find everything you can about them from websites, people who work there or know of the firm, and any other medium that you can do research. While it is important that you fit their needs, it is equally important that they fit yours as well. When you essentially view every hiring decision as finding the right fit for both the employer and employee, you will know not to be discouraged when it doesn't fit.
- Put yourself in the employer's role and go through the mental process of hiring yourself, based on your research into the needs of the company.
- Create a value profile for yourself which details your knowledge, experience, skills, characteristics, accomplishments, goals, and values. Similarly, create a profile for each prospective employer detailing their solutions, markets, mission, values, culture, and needs. Review these profiles to understand how your profile will fit each potential employer in a unique way.
- A great way to show that you fit is to secure a recommendation from an insider at the organization you want to work with. It's just as the old saying says, "it's not what you know, but who you know." However, I'll go further to say "it's not who you know, but who knows you and what they say about you."
- If there is a company you want to work for in the future, this will be a good long term strategy. Become the company's fan. Connect with them, call them, and build relationships with people who are already inside. Employers certainly prefer people who know and are fans of their products and services. If applicable and

timely, participate in their events, seek mentorship, or volunteer at their events. Let them know you are interested in being a part of their organization and they may share upcoming job openings. By the time this happens, you will have greater insight into their needs and also have insiders who will be your advocates. If you want to immediately work for that company, this strategy is risky as they may fill any open job before you apply. Consider this a long-term strategy.

- Create your student research project and interview the highest level person you can that is relevant to your research at the company you want to work with. This will give you access to a key contact with whom you can build a relationship and gain a deeper understanding of the prospective employer.

2) High Touch over High Tech

- Whenever possible, build relationships with the least amount of technology involved. Meet face to face, speak over the phone, and hand write your thank you note (and make sure to have handwritten signatures).
- Personally deliver your application to give you the opportunity to build a relationship with your prospective employer.

3) Effectively Market & Sell Yourself

- When possible, share a story instead of making a statement. For example, instead of stating that you are a hard worker, trustworthy, and a problem solver, share a story in which the listener will conclude that you have these characteristics. A compelling story might even lead the listener to infer even greater attributes than you intended. I once heard that people might forget what you say, but they will always remember how you make them feel. Understanding this and knowing too that stories drive more emotions than just statements when you can share a story, you will connect more with people and influence them.
- Your cover letter is a sale later or pitches to your prospective employer. Position yourself to be the person that is the best fit and quality for their needs. To do this effectively, make sure

you fully understand the needs they outlined in the job post. Share experiences and stories that convey your competence and character in your letter. Your letter should lead the reader to conclude that you are the right fit for their team and the right solution to their problem. When you do that, you will certainly get the opportunity to further sell your capabilities to them in an interview.

- Make your resume speak to the needs of the employer. Keep in mind that employers look at your resume to determine whether you have the experiences and skills necessary to meet their needs and solve their problems. You don't need to have the longest resume; you just need to demonstrate competence and range (competency, meaning you can do the work, and range, meaning you have greater value to grow and add to the employer). Furthermore, whatever you put on the resume, you should be excited to discuss during the interview. The last thing you want is to have the interviewer ask you about a resume item when you wish they had focused on something else. Leave out irrelevant details, or they may become a distraction. Finally, don't just list your history. With each entry, include a description of what you accomplished and your contributions. Share results so that your entries demonstrate your ability to produce results.

4) Be Creative & Stand Out

- Have a personal website that acts as an online resume that can be easily shared and reviewed. Make sure to update your LinkedIn Profile as many employers trust that profile as your resume.
- Make a video cover letter, resume, and professional online profile that can be easily viewed.
- Spend money to buy ads to market yourself to employers that you want to target.
- Position yourself as an authority. Volunteer to write for trade publications or any other mediums that can illustrate your expertise of a subject, or better yet, get them to pay you for submissions.

5) Lower or Reverse the Risk. If you can, make hiring you risk-free. (Use this strategy when there is a job position open which you want but have not yet proven your ability to succeed in. While you believe in your abilities, your prospective employer so far does not. This strategy gives you an opportunity to prove it.)

- Seek to add value before requesting value. Volunteer to give results before they hire you.
- Offer to work as an independent contractor to prove your ability to add value and solve specific problems they have. When they see your value, they agree to hire you full time as an employee.
- Accept a temporary position to get your foot in the door. Once they see you in action, they can better appreciate your skills and consider a full-time offer.

6) Your Network Is Your "Net Worth."

- Hiring people is all about knowing people. The more people that know you in a positive light, the more opportunities you will have. However, networking isn't a "just in time" act to connect with people when you need something. It is about you having many great relationships with people. These relationships are built and cultivated like a tree that you water and nurture over time. Networking is about you contributing to others, being a go-giver rather than a go-getter. Networking with people is fundamentally about connecting based on similar values and interests.
- Leverage online networks to expand your search for opportunities. However, make sure to update all your profiles to reflect your level of professionalism, especially your social media profiles. Employers often review your social media profiles to get a better perspective of you when considering you for hire.
- Leverage offline opportunities like job fairs to meet people face to face.
- Join associations that can further your knowledge but also expand your network of people. Many associations help members connect with each other and create opportunities to add value to each other. Every major industry has one or more

associations, which provide great networking opportunities through conferences, seminars, and forums. Many associations also have job databases that list career opportunities. Check out the association representing your field of interest, and look for local chapters in your area to join.

- Share your goal with others because you never know who they know. Often it is the second or even the third-degree relationships that can be your lucky break. We live in a small world after all.

7) Work with a Professional

- Many employers hire recruiters and headhunters to find the best candidates to fill their positions. It is advantageous to work with these professionals to learn their process, standards, and experiences. They may be able to connect you with a great employer who is looking for a person like you. In this case, the recruiter and headhunter are being paid by the employer.
- Consider hiring a professional, like a paid career advisor, to find you a fitting employer. In this case, you pay the professional to help you. Just make sure to research their service and try to negotiate pay based on their performance instead of time. This way, you don't pay unless and until they can perform for you.

8) Be Forward Thinking

- Identify problems that you can help solve. When you can identify an unmet need that the employer can use to grow his business and you can solve that need, you will successfully create a job for yourself.
- Don't decline the current offer or undervalue a current position if it is a stepping stone to another position that is available later within the organization. Continue to invest in yourself to increase your value, and then you can create the opportunity to advance within as an insider vs. being on the outside.
- Not all jobs are published publicly, so if you want to work at a certain place or for a certain employer, don't be afraid to ask and share your goals. Even if you don't think you qualify yet, many employers will hire for character and train for skill. Employers know that good people will always pay for themselves through the value they bring to the organization. Many employers have great training programs

so as long as you are a coachable person with a good character, you are a great candidate.

9) Be Human

- Be humble, sincere, and authentic. If you want to work at your dream company, go and share your dream with them and ask how you can prepare yourself to be able to work there in the future. Whatever they share, do it and keep in touch to update them. Build the relationship over time.
- Be open to professional growth. Do not limit yourself to only doing what you think you like now. More often than not, what you like to do now is what you are good at doing already – when you do it, you get a positive reaction that makes you feel good. Allow yourself to experience new challenges while you are young to grow and develop new knowledge and skills. As you develop these skills, you may also grow to like doing them and find an additional "passion."
- Be more interested than interesting by asking and listening more than talking. This is a great way to show that you are a caring human being that can work well with others. Great work is done in teams, so employers want people who can work with other people.
- Respect all people regardless of their title and position. Most often, the people who are key to your success are the assistants and receptionists. They are the gatekeepers and some of the most trusted people in the entire organization. To be respected is to show respect to all people.

10) Build Interviewing Skills

- The best way to practice interviewing is to play the part of the interviewer so you can understand their perspective and needs. After you have understood the mindset and needs of the interviewer, then practice being the interviewee.
- Record yourself to hear and see yourself. Ask a trusted mentor or advisor. Practice face to face interview and PHONE INTERVIEW skills. Often, I have great candidates that fail my phone interviews because they weren't prepared. Furthermore, I suggest practicing online video interviews as well as group interviews.

- Research behavioral interview questions to practice with as those are the most difficult for interviewees to answer yet the best questions for employers to ask. For example, one behavioral interview question is "Share with me a time where you had to make a difficult decision that was unpopular and how you handled it." Then, practice with questions specific to your industry as well as common interview questions.
- Remember that to effectively communicate, you not only need to focus on what you are saying but also how you are saying it. Often, HOW you say it is more important than WHAT you say.
- Be sincere and authentic. Everyone tries to "fit the mold." Being sincere and authentic rather than trying to fit in demonstrates confidence and professionalism. When possible, share stories to demonstrate experience and results but be mindful of timing and try not share a long story.

11) Earning a Promotion

- Increase your value by asking for and taking on more responsibility while delivering quality results. When you show that you can do the work of a higher position, you will naturally be recognized and be promoted to that position.
- Stay hungry and humble to learn more. You get opportunities for promotion as you develop more knowledge and skill.
- Ask your employer for feedback and ways to improve. This will give direction on areas for improvement so you can become more valuable. The goal is to become better every day.
- Attend training workshops, seminars, and personal and professional development courses to build skills.

Performance-based Income Strategies.

Performance-based income depends on the person's time and performance. Some examples are commissions, bonuses, contract pay, profit draws, and profit sharing. In this section, I review strategies to maximize your performance-based income via commissions or bonuses, contracts, and recurring business profits.

Strategies for Pure Performance Pay Only (Commissions and Bonuses)

When you know your individual earning power is high and can quickly learn and adapt to new processes and systems, take full advantage of pure performance pay opportunities such as jobs that pay commission only. Since you are taking all the income risk, your time investment will be the biggest cost to you if the opportunity doesn't set you up for success in producing results and making money. Because you are paid on your performance, you need to be strategic with your decision. The following are strategies to use when you are being paid on pure performance only.

- Select an opportunity that gives you best-in-class training programs and the best platform to succeed. Remember, you assume financial risk because your employer doesn't pay you anything until you make them money. In exchange, they need to invest in developing your knowledge and skills. Thus, the worst case for you is that you trade your time for free training and learning – in other words, you receive free professional development.

- Think and do big. Since most performance pay is based on a percentage of sales or profit sharing, get involved with industries where the volume is larger or the sales price is higher. For example, you can choose to make 20% on a $100 sale or 3% on a $100,000 sale or 1% on a $1,000,000 sale. Examples of these industries are real estate and selling businesses.

- While your performance as a "producer" is limited to you, your results can increase significantly when you act as a "leader" or "trainer" to other producers and create exponential income through profit sharing with each producer you lead or train. The better you train and lead an ever growing number of people, the more money you can make.

When you choose to earn income based on your performance, you assume the risk, because when you don't perform, you won't earn. Below are strategies that can help you lower your risk and provide more income stability while preserving income potential with high commission pays.

- Negotiate with an employer to pay you beyond your hourly or salary rate when you can deliver measurable performances beyond your primary responsibility. For example, if you primarily do customer service, but you are also effective at upselling the customers you service, ask to be included in a sales-related commission program.

- If you are offered commission only, negotiate for a base hourly pay plus commission that is based on your results. For example, if your average performance-based pay is $3,000 per month over a certain period, negotiate a "floor" near that amount so that your income doesn't fluctuate too much between the months, especially when you have bills that need to be paid on a consistent basis. This becomes important when you take on more life and financial responsibilities such as having a family of your own that depends on your ability to produce consistent income. Be open to a lower base amount than your average, but remember that it is simply a safety net in bad months. Be fair and work with your employer to review your performance regularly to adjust the compensation to be most fair for both. The key to this strategy is to set regular performance reviews ahead of time and to set clear expectations to avoid any negative feelings of unfairness.

- Think beyond cash payment for your performance related pay. Many organizations, especially startups, may offer stock options to attract and retain talent. Stock options give the recipient the ability to purchase ownership shares of the company at a set price. The recipient makes money by exercising the option and selling the stock at a market price higher than the price they paid. Early employees of Google, Facebook, Microsoft, and Snapchat become multi-millionaires and even billionaires overnight when their companies' stocks "went public" (became available to the general public to purchase on stock exchanges), and the market price rose well above the option price. One interesting feature of stock options is that both the employer and the employee assume a risk of income because the income is tied to the overall performance of the company. If the company doesn't become valuable, the stock options are worthless. On the other hand, if the company does become valuable, the monetary value of the exercised options can be enormous.

Strategies for Independent Contractors

A recent study estimates that by 2020, 40% of Americans will become independent contractors.[22] In this arrangement, organizations contract with independent workers for short-term projects, engagements, or gigs. Many contracts can be renewed, leading to long-term arrangements, but there are no guarantees. Because of this trend, the term used to describe this new economy of independent contractors performing various gigs is the "gig economy." Additionally, with online platforms, anybody can work anywhere for anyone and get paid instantly at any time of day. People are no longer limited to working locally and physically. The marketplace is now the entire world.

To get the best contract gigs at the best rates, I will discuss the following strategies for you.

1) Have a Business Mindset

- Working for yourself first begins with your mindset. No longer do you have someone else to hold you accountable, so you must be your own boss and stay on track to produce results. If you are undisciplined, learn how to become disciplined.
- You are officially in business for yourself, so think like a business owner. Over time, as you develop more skills and experience, you can then truly be a business owner with teams of people, systems, and processes to support you. I'll cover that in the next section.
- Follow the best practices of successful business. Don't let your small business make you small-minded. Study the largest and most successful businesses that relate to what you are doing independently and learn from them.
- Set up a proper business financial accounting system to keep good records. There are plenty of free online and offline programs – be resourceful and pick one you can understand and that gives you results. (It doesn't make sense for me to suggest one here as there isn't a program that fits all needs.) Your business needs to have accurate financial statements– remember the income statement and balance sheet. By keeping track of your numbers, you can make more effective business decisions.

- Open a business bank account separate from your personal bank account. It is a best business practice to have your business and personal money separated, especially to show organizations like the IRS that you keep proper financial accounts.
- Have proper insurance protection according to your business risk exposure. For example, if you drive for Uber, make sure to have the necessary coverage to protect you and your customers.
- Consider setting up a business entity such as an S-corporation or a limited liability company (LLC) to maximize tax deductions to increase your net income. While you can still deduct business expenses without setting yourself up as a legal business entity, the IRS may deny the deduction if it considers your contract work a hobby. With a business entity, there are multiple legal ways to reduce your tax bill. Work with a qualified attorney and tax professional to help you do this legally and properly.
- To brand yourself or position yourself professionally, register your business with your state or county. Check with your state or governmental office for their process.

2) Do Marketing

- Depending on your type of self-employment, you may need to build up your brand or professional reputation. Being self-employed, your brand and reputation can mean the difference between commanding low, average, or above-average pay. Most often, your brand is your first impression, so your business name, logos, and profile should be consistent with how you want your clients to feel about you. In the end, it is all about establishing trust so to keep that in mind, frequently ask yourself whether you would choose yourself over the alternatives if you were the client.
- Be clear on what you are, what you do, what you are not, and what you don't do. If it is difficult for you to explain to people quickly what you do and the value that you provide, you may be wasting your time and money with marketing. Take the time to know what makes you unique and what competitive advantage you have so that others cannot or have a hard time competing with you.
- Be clear on who your customers are. There is a difference between customers and consumers. Customers pay you while consumers

use your products and services. By knowing who to target your marketing efforts toward, you will be more effective.

- Leverage free marketing whenever possible. Use social connections and word of mouth marketing to spread the message of your products and services.

- Use social media to expand your marketing reach. However, don't use every social media platform. Focus on the channels where you know the users, your target customers, will most likely be in the position to want to know and use your products and services. For example, if you are a home interior designer, use Houzz. If you offer business-related services, use LinkedIn. If you offer consumer products or services, use Facebook. If you offer video and photography, use YouTube and Pinterest.

- Build a portfolio, client list, or book of business that you can use to prove and demonstrate your competency to prospects and potential customers.

- Have a website or blog or internet home base that others can learn more about you and connect with you.

- Leverage your competitors by partnering with them. Especially in the service business, there are times when you or your competitors are unavailable, so the best marketing you can get is for them to recommend you. Certainly, you should do the same for them when you are unavailable.

- Maintain marketing momentum. Even while you are busy working and serving lots of customers, you need to keep marketing, or else you may not have work once you finish with your current customers. When you have the good problem of too many customers to handle, that's a good time to partner with others (with a profit sharing arrangement, of course) or begin hiring people to build a team. This is when you advance beyond self-employed to a true business owner. I'll go into detail in the next section.

- Effective management requires measurement. Track and measure your marketing return on investment. How much net profit are you producing from your marketing? Setup Key Performance Indicators (KPI) such as average cost per customer acquisition, which gives you how much money you spend to gain each new customer. If your average profit per customer is $100, but your average cost per customer acquisition is $110, you are losing $10 per customer. At this point, you have three options: increase the profit per customer, reduce the cost per acquisition, or create a long-term profit strategy that increases the lifetime value of the customer with repeat businesses or referrals.

- Turn existing customers into your marketers and advocates. Since they already know your quality product and service, they are your best marketers. Referrals allow you to grow your customer base exponentially without increasing marketing cost.

- Check in with your past customers. You don't need to find a treasure map – I am letting you know now that your treasure is your past customers. Create a way to stay connected with them and continue to build relationships with them. This is where Customer Relationship Management (CRM) software helps.

- Network and join associations to meet new people and make in-person connections. Don't be overly high tech and forget we are all humans. High touch beats high tech in one-on-one competition.

3) Price Strategically

- Know your value and the value you create for your customers. Pricing is often misunderstood by both the buyer and the provider. The buyer may think that higher price indicates higher quality when that is not always true. The provider may think that by lowering their prices, they attract more customers – but that is not always true either. Price is what a person pays but value is what he receives. Focus on the value when discussing and negotiating prices so both buyer and seller can find a fair price. But remember that it is the provider's responsibility to communicate the value to the customer. The most direct way to understand your value as a provider and to develop effective communications is to ask the past and current customers to share with you the value they perceived. It is the most authentic value description you can find to share with others.

- Set bundles and packages to make decisions easier for the buyer and also for the producer. For a creative person, it can seem natural to customize a service for each customer, but having too many options makes it difficult for the customer to decide. For example, if you are a graphic artist, instead of asking the customer what format they want, what size they need, and how many prints they want, create packages A, B, and C that meet most customer's needs and are profitable for you. This way, it is easy for customers to work with you, and you don't have to customize your services for every customer. Win-win.

- Research your customer's alternative options and the associated costs. If they don't hire you, for example, they might have to hire a local employee with less experience at a higher cost. The cost of a company to find, hire, and train a new employee is much higher than using an independent contractor. Companies may need to pay taxes, payroll services, and benefits to their employees. The value you offer as an independent contractor is that you can be their plug-and-play solution to their immediate need. Having information on your cost relative to the alternatives increases your confidence to keep your service price high and fair.

- Consider offering a discount if the customer may become a great source of leads for additional customers. For example, if you have the opportunity to work for an influential company or celebrity, that customer might introduce you to many more clients. Working with high-profile clients is also a great portfolio and resume builder.

- Don't be afraid to charge extra for incidental and incremental work. Remember you are building a relationship with your customers, so it is important to be up-front in setting expectations. Let them understand that you are willing to negotiate pricing and scope if the project becomes larger and more complex. Or you may choose to keep the same price, but let your client know that you provided extra services because of the trust and long-term relationship that you want to build with them.

- You can fire your customer or charge them a fee for being a bad customer. Being self-employed, you are the boss, so you can choose who you want to work with. If your customer is causing a problem or you feel that this customer is a potential problem, factor that into your pricing by increasing it to make it worth your time.

- Keep free work or volunteer work to a minimum. There are times when you need to work for free to get yourself in the door because you have not yet proven yourself. Don't put ego in the way of success. Free work might give you access to new markets, new networks, or new opportunities, but it must be clear that you are doing it as a limited promotion; otherwise, you become known as the free resource and lower your value. I have a mentee who built a very successful videography business by offering his service to schools in exchange for permission to promote his business name and contact information at the end of the video he created, which was distributed to all students, faculty, and alumni.

- Ask for partial payment up front. While you may trust your client to pay you when you deliver, you need some proof that they have the financial ability and intent.

4) Specialize

- Specializing in a particular area or skill set is a way to earn instant trust because you position yourself as an expert. While you can do many other things, when the customer is focused on their problem, they just need the best person to solve their immediate problem. They need someone with that specific skill, so being a specialist gives you credibility and trust.
- Research the skills that are required and needed for various industries, and align your skill sets with those industries that you know value your specialty.
- Keep your skills sharp and updated to maintain your expert position.

5) Perform

- Provide regular performance updates and set regular meetings to keep the relationship going and maintain trust. The more you learn about your customer's needs and problems, the more value you can provide by positioning yourself as the solution. Not only do regular performance updates reassure your client and maintain their trust in you, but they also offer an opportunity for you to learn about other problems and needs that you can offer to solve with additional projects. This can mean more money for you and longer-term income.
- Leverage software and technology to make you effective and productive. Use industry specific software when it exists, like customer relationship management software (CRM) to keep you and your customer on track with the project.

6) Bidding on Projects with Online Platforms

- To make it easy for people and companies to find the best contract providers, many online marketplaces exist that connect the two. The most popular one I use is Upwork. I recommend you do your research to find marketplaces and platforms that may be specific to your targeted industry. By using a platform, contract providers don't have to market themselves to find customers. Instead, they bid and send proposals for specific projects, and they can be hired and paid within the platform. The following strategies are designed to help you win more contracts on Upwork or similar platforms. Certainly, there is a fee to use the platform, but the fee is minimal and should be looked at relative to your success.

- Focus on one or two platforms and understand them. Read the user guides and study how other successful contractors bid and craft proposals.

- Become a user of that platform as the "employer." Create a real project that you are capable of doing yourself. This way, you can see how others bid for these services and also judge the quality of your competitors' work. By going through the entire process of awarding a project to another contractor, you learn how to effectively manage each step of the project as the contractor.

- Have a profile that you, yourself, would want to hire. Your profile is often the first impression your clients will have of you. Make it an impression you want them to have. Don't leave it to chance.

- Don't let the customer's budget limit your bid. Upwork requires all project posted to have a budget, but many clients don't have a firm budget, so they post a low number to avoid overpaying. As a client, I often don't have a set budget, and I frequently award projects above my posted budget when I am convinced the independent contractor is more than worth it. I respect those who bid more because it indicates that they value their time and the quality of their services. These contractors choose me as much as I choose them.

- In your profile and your proposals, share your experience in terms of results you have gotten for other similar customers, not in terms of years. Don't just give your age. Don't just give the years you have been working in an industry. These facts don't communicate the results you can provide or the value you have to offer. You can be a genius kid with little experience in an industry but know you can do the work because you have done similar projects (even as homework or for fun) and gotten results. Of course, don't say to the client that you did it for homework and you have no experience, just focus on the problem that the customer describes and focus on proving you can do it in a way that is convincing. Address how your specific knowledge, experience, skills, and credentials will help them solve their need in ways that no other contractor can.

- Quality over quantity. Don't just send proposals and bids all day long. Only bid and send proposals to projects you really know you can do and are really interested in. When you send the proposal, it should be customized to that project's need. Address every concern, question, and the points rose in the original post. Read between the lines of the post to know how concerned or worried the customer is with the problem they have as well as the level of urgency. Try to gauge the communication style of the customer to respond in a way that showcases your skills. For example, if you are a copywriter, your response is an example of your copywriting skills, so treat every word as if your contract depends on it.

- Be professional but relatable and human. Although you are the supposed expert, be humble and do not use an arrogant tone. Your customer needs your skills and not your judgment of them for not being able to do what you can do. Your customer must be able to talk to you and trust you. They must feel that you are approachable.

- Your first goal is to get the client to communicate with you – ideally, to send you a message. A project may get 50 to 100 bids, and there won't be enough time for the client to interview every bidder, so take advantage of every message and communication opportunity. Whether a customer offers an interview or not, let them know you are open to any form of interview. I prefer phone interviews, so I view it as a plus when a contractor is open to that.

- Don't skip any additional questions they include in the post. Again, treat all questions as golden opportunities to share how you can solve their problem and add value. Always think of how you would want a question answered if you were the one to ask it.

- Be concise but not too short. Get to the point. Write just enough to answer their preliminary questions and deliver your value proposition.

Strategies for Recurring Business Profits (Building Systems, Teams, and Processes)

This section of performance pay is different from contract pay in that it addresses an income stream that may not require or be limited to one person's time. You will learn about business development. When you invest in building a business that isn't just you operating it, you can be one step closer to achieving financial freedom. The key is to invest in systems, processes, and people. The more effective you are at developing businesses, the more profits you can draw from it.

I love building businesses, and over the past decade, I have had great opportunities to find amazing mentors and hire the best consultants to help me become better as an owner, CEO, and business developer. As they have helped me, I want to help you. I call this "The 5Ps of Business Development."

The 5Ps are: People, Positioning, Product, Promotion, and Profits

1) **People**

    Your business is only as good as its people. Even if you operate a business that has no employees but uses independent contractors, your business is only as good as the contractors you hire to do the work. Business is all about people. Henry Ford, the founder of the Ford Motor Company, the creator of the mass production assembly line, and the seventh-wealthiest figure of the modern period[23] said it best, "You can take my factories, burn up my buildings, but give me my people and I'll build the business right back again." The key objectives are:

    - Don't go cheap on hiring people, as good people pay for themselves
    - The best investment a company can make is offering its people opportunities for personal and professional development
    - Treat your people like family as you are likely to spend as much or more time with them as your family members.

- Hire for character, and then train for skill. Skills can be trained, culture and personal values cannot.
- Hire slowly, but fire quickly. You will make mistakes in choosing people. Be quick to recognize that and remove that person before it affects your business.
- Trust, but verify. Hold your people accountable. Each one should know exactly how and when you evaluate their performance.
- Ask your employees to set monthly goals, and work with them to achieve those goals. Don't set the bar so low that it doesn't foster growth, but don't set it so high that it becomes unrealistic.
- Don't immediately assume your employee is at fault when something goes wrong. Ask and try to understand whether it was due to a lack of resources, a mistake, or another reason. Don't lose good people for the wrong reasons.
- Keep improving yourself. The key in having great people is you. Being the top person means that you must continuously invest in yourself to become better. If you, the person at the top, don't become better, the company will not become better. Invest in growing your knowledge and skills through books, workshops, seminars, and private coaching. The best only want to work with the best, so you need to be a person worthy of having great people work with you.

2) **Positioning**

Business value depends partly on how the company is positioned. The same coffee can be sold for $1 or $4 depending on how it is positioned. Coffee can just be coffee, or it can be a cultural brand identity. This is the difference between your standard coffee shop and Starbucks. The key objectives are:

- Position your business as a necessity, not a commodity. Provide unique value to your customers to meet a need that isn't being met elsewhere. For example, a boutique restaurant could offer a menu that is unlike any other restaurant in the area, meeting their customers' need for budget-friendly burritos or casual French fare.
- Be known for something that customers can easily discuss with others. That increases your referral business.

- Be polarizing. To have true fans, you need to stand for something that is meaningful and strong. Of course, having strong convictions attracts critics as well as fans. However, if you choose to be neutral, you choose to be average. For example, look at clothing brands. The most successful brands know what they stand for and what they don't.
- Give customers a reason to be your customer, fan, or advocate. What are the stories, values, and missions that connect with your customers?
- Don't compete, create. Make your positioning irrelevant to your competition. A shoe can provide protection for your feet, make a fashion statement, or signal a social identity. It depends on how you position the shoe to your customers. Thus, you don't have to compete, but rather create a new positioning for your products. Consider repositioning your car delivery service as a mobile advertising billboard, for example. You can earn advertising money for the ads you put on your car while making deliveries. The chances are high that you make more money positioning yourself as a mobile advertising billboard.

3) **Product**

Great products and services market themselves. Once a customer experiences it, he spreads the word. This is the essence of billion dollar businesses and brands: the product markets itself. Apple, Facebook, Snapchat, Twitter, and Amazon are all examples of successes in this area. The key objectives are:

- Create products and services that market themselves. Customers use them repeatedly and refer them to others. This is the best and fastest way to grow effectively.
- Create a product that solves a truly unmet need.
- The best products and services do one or all of the following well: save time, save money, and save the hassle.
- Let your mind be your product factory. Digital products are most profitable and offer high scalability. Think of software, apps, eBooks, online courses, and mobile games.
- Source deep and wide. Sourcing your product and managing your supply chain can make or break your business. When you

are unable to secure the product(s) in time for your busy selling season, your business may not only miss the opportunity to sell but also be stuck with cash tied up in inventory.

- Price effectively. A 1% increase in price may result in a 100% increase in net profit. For example, you increase the price of your product from $100 to $101. If your net profit was $1 before, the price increase could double your net profit to $2. This is an oversimplified example, but I want to make you understand how important it is for you to price your products at the optimum level of supply and demand. An example of how just a fraction of a penny increase can be worth millions, if not billions, is the gasoline business. Look carefully at the price of a gallon. It is $X.YZ 9/10. Notice the 9/10, which is 9/10 of a penny more per gallon. So if the gallon is $2.00 9/10, it is actually 2.009. That small fraction of a penny, multiplied by millions of gallons pumped per year is a large net profit.

4 Promotion

The strategies for marketing I shared for independent contractors are also effective for businesses. This section builds upon the power of promotion to scale a business.

The key objectives are:

- Leverage partnerships. Bill Gates made Microsoft successful by partnering with IBM to put Windows on IBM computers. With partnerships, you can piggyback on existing distribution channels to quickly grow your business.
- Plan out your calendar with specific marketing campaigns that are best for months, seasons, and holidays. It is common for big businesses to have their marketing calendar planned out years in advance. Some businesses, such as department stores, even require that of their suppliers
- Study your closest 10 to 20 competitors, and figure out how to position your product or service better than they do. Know who they serve, what pricing they have, their unique value position, and their weakness.

- Your business needs a story. Stories connect and relate to people on a deep level so they remember the brand much more effectively. Buying decisions are driven by emotions more than logic, so marketing messages should have a story.

5 Profit

Operational excellence drives net profit for a business. The best examples are Walmart and McDonalds. Both of these businesses are able to sell products at low prices while maintaining healthy bottom-line profits for the business. There are many businesses that need to be operating at world-class levels independent of people, products , and financial management. Businesses that can produce income for you consistently and independently by nature need to have great processes and systems.

The key objectives are:

- Financial accounting systems and processes are critical to knowing how and where to improve profits. Think of flying a plane without accurate instruments to give you key readings and numbers. Have the best people crunch the numbers and build your financial systems. Going cheap here can result in you not having the information to grow your business, just as hiring the cheapest people makes it difficult for a business to achieve financial success.
- Keep some profits in the bank to support the business during bad times or times of rapid expansion. Bad times can mean little to no sales, when you need cash to sustain operations. During expansion phases, you need enough cash to support the additional investment. Both bad and good times can cause a business to run out of cash and go out of business.
- Marketing is a great way to get the phones ringing, attract visitors to your website, and bring people into your store, but if your people and operations fail to convert them into paying customers, your business breaks down. It doesn't make sense to spend more money on marketing if the problem lies with the operations and processes.
- Automate repetitive processes to increase consistency and productivity.

- Leverage technology and digital tools. Research the best resources that your industry-leading competitors are using and model after them.
- Learn from the best practices of other businesses like yours. These best practices include but not limited to: business positioning and strategy, sales and marketing, operational management, human resource management, financial and accounting systems, revenue model and structure, systems and software, and legal structure. Instead of repeating the mistakes of the past entrepreneurs, learn from them and build upon what they have built so you can be better and greater. You can learn best practices from books and online research, or by participating in industry associations. Just know that best practices are constantly being updated to reflect the new processes, systems, and structures. To ensure business success, make sure to start with a solid foundation that is flexible enough to adapt, adjust, and advance forward.

The 5Ps for Business Development discussed here is just a brief overview to give you a foundation for developing your business. I encourage you to seek a qualified mentor to help you further.

Investment-Based Income Strategies

As I have shared with you, there are two ways in which investments earn money for you: producing income or creating capital gains. Since this is the income section, I only discuss income-producing investments here. Because investments are recorded as assets on the balance sheet, and Chapter 6 of this book is dedicated to discussing Assets, I discuss investments in more detail in that chapter. The following is an overview of investments that can provide passive income for you. The term used to describe these investments is "passive income" investments.

1) U.S. Treasuries

For this investment, you lend money to the US government who pays you back with interest. The risk is low, so the potential return on investment (ROI) is low.

2) Certificates of Deposit (CD)

For this investment, you can go to a bank or credit union and buy their savings certificate. Each CD gives you a fixed interest rate for a specific period, usually from 3 months to years. The longer the duration (time) is, the higher the rate for you. The rates are low compared to other investment options, but CDs are secured by the federal government through the Federal Deposit Insurance Corporation (FDIC). The risks are low so expect a low return. For every 1% interest it may pay you a year, you could earn $1,000 on a $100,000 investment.

3) Bonds

For this investment, you lend money to businesses or governments, who pay you back what you lent to them plus interest. Often the interest payment to you is every six months. Expect a range of interest rates, as the rate depends on how much risk there is of the business or government default. Like us individuals have credit scores to determine how risky we are, companies and governments have credit ratings. The higher the credit rating of the business and government, the lower the risk of default, and the lower the interest rate paid. A great reason to invest in US government bonds is to earn tax-free interest income.

4) Dividend Yielding Stocks

For this investment, you are buying share(s) of stock of a publicly traded company that pays dividends to its shareholders. Not all companies pay dividends, so you must do your research. Usually, companies that pay dividends are mature, well-established firms that don't need to reinvest all of their profits back into the business to grow but can afford to share the profits by distributing them to shareholders in the form of dividends. The dividend percentage will change based on risk so do your research as always. Keep in mind too that when the stock price goes up (appreciates in value), you can sell the stock to earn a capital gain. However, because this section only addresses passive income, the way to do so is to hold the stock to generate dividend income, which is usually paid quarterly (every three months).

5)   Renting Real Estate

For this investment, you are buying real estate and renting it. This is one of most effective and best-loved investment choices. You can either hire a property manager to manage the rental to make it more of a "passive" investment or chose to do it yourself. Even if you manage it yourself, there is relatively little ongoing involvement once you have a renter in your unit that is paying you monthly. Depending on the purchase price and rental price, your return on investment ranges from 2% to 12% or higher. In addition to the income generation from real estate, what makes it a favorite for many investors is that it also gives the investor tax benefits as well such as deductions to pay lower taxes. In this section, we only focus on creating recurring income, so in chapter 6, you will also learn how real estate can be sold when it appreciates in value to generate capital gains.

6)   Buy Real Estate Indirectly through Real Estate Investment Trusts
(REITs)

For this investment, you are buying shares of a fund that uses the collective capital of all investors to buy larger, more complex real estate. With this, you can access real estate sectors such as large commercial complexes, hospitals, and shopping malls without actually owning them directly. REITs are similar to dividend yielding stocks, which pays out a percentage of company profits to their shareholders, but different in that REITs pay the majority of their profits (90%) to shareholders. As with other investments noted in this section, you can also earn capital gains if you sell shares when the price per share appreciates.

7)   Annuities

For this investment, you give a financial institution such as a bank or an insurance company a sum of money up front, with an agreement that they will pay you a steady stream of income for a set period. The payment stream can begin immediately or be delayed until a later time. The amount earned per month depends on the answers to the three questions below, but the key understanding is that the more time you give the annuity provider to invest, the more money they agree to pay you monthly.

- How much are you giving them today?
- When do you want them to start paying you (remember that you can elect to have them start immediately or years later)?
- Are any specific guarantees included, such as beating inflation?

8) Private Equity

For this investment, you invest into privately held (as opposed to public) companies, often new startup companies. For example, imagine when Facebook, Google, or Snapchat were starting that you had the opportunity to invest in them. The return on investment is potentially huge, but it is also a very high risk because of the high failure rates of startups. Furthermore, your investment is "locked up" with additional capital investments "called" (required by the manager) over a long period. Let's say you are Harvard University and you commit $5B to a PE fund. They might call $1M in year one, nothing in year two, then $3M at the beginning of year three, then another $1M in the middle of year three, and then you're locked for the remainder. As an investor, you have to manage the capital calls as well as your investments themselves, and you must make sure you have liquid assets to meet them. Furthermore, private investments are possible, but difficult to access. It may require you to be an accredited investor, and even then, you may not be selected by the private equity manager for the opportunity. In the United States, being an accredited investor means that you must have a net worth of at least $1,000,000 or have made at least $200,000 in each of the past two years and expect to continue to do so in the current year. However, if you want it badly enough and are aware of it now, you can do it with proper planning and preparation.

9) Crowdfunding

For this investment, you are investing with a group of other investors. Here are a few options.

- **Peer to Peer Lending via Online Platforms:** Many online platforms are available, so do your research and seek professional advice. Examples are Upstart, Funding Circle, Prosper Marketplace, CircleBack Lending, Peerform, SoFi, and Lending Club. Each has specific requirements, and the ROI can be low or high, from 4% to above 35%, all depending on how much risk you want to take and which platform you use. Remember, high ROI means a high risk of getting nothing and losing your money too.
- **Crowdfunding for Business Start Ups:** This is similar to private equity investment. Keep in mind that these are private investments, so they are not as liquid as publicly traded investments. You may be required to be an accredited investor.
- **Real estate crowdfunding:** Similar to REITs investments, with real estate crowdfunding you can invest in real estate without owning it directly. REITs have higher fees while real estate crowdfunding may require you to be an accredited investor. Again, these opportunities are subject to availability in your market, and I strongly encourage seeking professional financial guidance when you invest in anything.

10) Invest in Creating & Selling Your Own Products and Services

For this investment, you are in control of your own products and services as well as how much return on investment you earn. Since this section is "passive" income, I will focus on products and services that earn you income without you actively working for it. Here is a quick list of products that you can create once and automatically sell it over and over again to provide you with a steady stream of income.

- Books
- Software
- Apps
- Music
- Photography
- Online content such as videos, articles, and info courses.

Benefit-Based Income Strategies

Benefit Income comes from family, government, and other sources, such as student scholarships. In this section, I will show you how you can access government benefit programs and student scholarships. Family benefit income comes from love, so just make sure to show your appreciation and love back. The best thank you to family is to succeed in your life and be a good human being that family can be proud of.

I will begin with information on accessing government benefit programs. To learn more about each of these programs, please visit your government websites with a ".gov" at the end. The one I used is usa.gov. However, before I begin, I want to share a few instances where I accidentally overheard parents discussing how they preferred not to work and instead chose to stay poor so they could continue to qualify for government assistance. These programs are need-based, but many want to stay in the position of need. This thinking to me is quicksand: it pulls you down slowly until when you want to get out, you no longer can because you are in too deep. It is much harder to get out, and your mind gives up in the process.

Growing up, my father told me to become an independent person who is in the position to help other people. While our family needed government assistance when we first immigrated to America as refugees, my father explained to me that aid should only be temporary. It was my responsibility to go out on my own as quickly as possible and become financially independent. The goal for me was to quickly disqualify for aid and not let free aid money become the poison pill that limited my potential.

However, there are times when government support and temporary aid can propel you forward and up. Don't let ego and pride prevent you from receiving help. Be gracious and use it to build upon it. Just don't let yourself depend on it. When you do qualify, the following are the types of potential government programs that can offer you help:

1) **Affordable Housing.**

These programs can help with renting or buying an affordable place to live.

2) Healthcare.

Both federal and state level programs may help with your healthcare.

3) Food Assistance.

These programs help you buy nutritious food for you and your family.

4) Grants and Loans.

These are federal and state level programs that give you loans and grants for various purposes, including starting your own small business.

5) Help with Bills.

Learn about government programs that help pay bills and other expenses.

6) Programs and Benefits for Active Military.

For our heroes, there are benefits and assistance available to military members and their families at federal and state levels.

7) Retirement.

There are government retirement programs and pension benefits for qualified people.

8) Social Security.

This is a federal insurance program that provides benefits to retired people and those who are unemployed or disabled with no income.

9) Unemployment Benefits.

These programs and resources help the temporarily unemployed.

10) Financial Aid for Students.

These programs help students afford college so they can become more valuable and increase the overall human capital value of our country.

Most often, financial aid will not be enough to cover college costs, and many families will not even qualify for financial aid. The best way to earn money for college is through scholarships. I personally relied on scholarships to help pay for college, and I even got enough cash scholarships to buy a car and start my business. I also have a few friends who received over $1 million dollars in scholarships.

Here are key strategies to earning scholarship money for college.

- **Search & Ask Early.**

    Many scholarships go unawarded each year. Students need to begin their search early and plan out their calendar year(s) in advance. I suggest you start one year in advance at a minimum, but two years is ideal. Don't wait until senior year to search, when there is more competition and many scholarship opportunities have already passed. Senior year can also be stressful with college applications, so there is much to distract you from scholarship opportunities. For example, the Horatio Alger Scholarship's current deadline to apply is early in the school year in October. If school starts in August, it means the student only has two months, assuming he didn't start early. If you start your research early enough, you can review and learn from previous winners and even practice applying for it. Download and complete the application, but then ask your mentors to review it. By the time you truly apply, you only need to update it based on the feedback you received and submit it. This way, you can have more time to apply for scholarships that are time-intensive and may dissuade other students. Also, planning ahead allows you to submit many more applications. In your search for scholarships, use the internet and begin making a list. The internet gives you many options, so begin organizing each scholarship by the application deadline and put them all in your master calendar. Away from the internet are local scholarships that are only advertised through your local community organizations such as YMCA, Kiwanis, Rotary, Elks Club, and Boys & Girls Club. Visit the organizations' websites or offices to find out. Then, go to your city hall and ask for your city's list of scholarships. Finally, ask your scholar counselor, who has a treasure trove of scholarships that past students from your school have won.

- **Apply Authentically.**

Scholarships have many applicants. If your essays are generic and lack authenticity, they will quickly be rejected. To be authentic and sincere, don't just use adjectives to describe yourself such as "I am dedicated," "I am hard working," and "I am awesome." Instead, share experiences and stories that demonstrate these abilities and allow the reader to infer that you are "dedicated, hardworking, and awesome."

- **Submit a Professional Application.**

Before submitting, make sure you have reviewed everything and have given it to a mentor or advisor to make sure that you are not missing any requirements. Many good applications are disqualified for being incomplete. Don't forget to answer each question, and attach every form. Make a copy of everything in case it is lost, damaged, or misdelivered. When you submit it via standard mail, use packaging that ensures it will be protected from the elements. Finally, send the application by certified mail, return receipt requested or with delivery confirmation.

- **Know Its True Value.**

The money is great, but the potential for mentorships and network relationships is even more valuable. Become a great scholar of the organization by making sure you succeed with the money awarded to you. Success means you achieve your goal and become a person that will carry the spirit of servant-leadership and give back to others.

How Income Tax Affects Your Pay

Since tax is a Liability and Chapter 7 is dedicated to discussing Liabilities, I will not go into all the details of tax here. Because it is important for you to understand at this time how tax affects your income, here, I will help you with what to expect from your first paycheck.

If you haven't received your first paycheck yet, the experience will be an unforgettable one. Yes, it is very exciting to get paid and earn your first paycheck, but in addition to that excitement, you will quickly learn that you must pay your share of taxes. I apologize in advance if I ruin this surprise – feel free to skip this section if you want to be surprised. If you want to know and be prepared, let's look at a paycheck together.

Your Exciting Paycheck			
Annual Gross Pay	$60,000.00	**Bi-weekly Gross Pay (Annual / 26)**	$2,307.69
Tax Year	2017	**Required Deductions**	
Pay Frequency	Bi-weekly	**Federal Tax Withholding**	-$390.91
Federal Filing Status	Single	**Social Security**	-$143.08
Federal Exemptions	0	**Medicare**	-$33.46
Additional Withholding	0	**State Tax**	-$110.83
State	California	**SDI**	-$20.77
Allowances	0		
CA SDI	Yes	**Net Bi-weekly Pay**	*$1,608.64*

Required Deductions

Every person working in the United States is to pay certain taxes. To make sure they get paid, the money is withheld (taken out of) your wages each paycheck. The amount withheld is based on the size of your salary and the information on the W-4 form you file with your employer. The W-4 is a form that employees fill out that gives information about their marital status, number of exemptions, allowances, and dependents claimed, and other factors. Based on that information, it gives the employer the correct amount of tax to withhold from an employee's paycheck. Changes to the W-4 can be made at any time, and they can result in the employer withholding more or less tax.

- **Federal & State Income Tax:** Amount varies based on where you live, and the deductions and exemptions claimed on your W-4 form. You can do a quick online search to find out your current federal and state income tax rates.
- **Medicare Tax:** Funds health insurance for Americans age 65 and older. This is a set percentage, for example, 1.45% for 2017.
- **Social Security Tax:** Funds Social Security for American seniors and disabled people. This is a set percentage, for example, 6.2% for 2017.
- **SDI (State Disability Insurance):** Only in certain states, this funds disability benefits for people who can't work due to injury or other disability.

Voluntary Deductions

- **Medical, dental, and vision insurance:** This premium you pay for the insurance coverage you elected to have.
- **Retirement Benefits (401k or other):** An account you set up with your employer to save pre-tax money for retirement. You will learn about this in more detail in chapter 6.
- **Life Insurance:** This is the premium payment for the policy that will pay a death benefit to your stated beneficiary upon your death. This option is only available if the employer offers it.
- **Disability Insurance:** This is an insurance policy that will pay you if you become disabled due to illness or injury. This option is only available if the employer offers it.
- **Other Deductions:** Other Health care options, stock plans, and other retirement options may be listed here.

In the example shown above, this worker only had the required deductions (on the left-hand side), which totaled $705.29. These deductions reduced the amount of gross pay from $2307.69 to the net pay of $1602.40. "Gross" is the full amount before deduction and "net" is the final (take-home) amount after all deductions.

Bi-weekly sounds like it is paid twice a week, but it is actually every other week.

How Income Tax Affects Self-Employment Income

When you employ yourself, it is easy to forget that you need to also pay income taxes on your self-employment income. Unlike working as an employee of a company and having taxes deducted from your paycheck automatically, the self-employed need to do these themselves. Please consult your tax professional for details, as I am just providing a reference guide to help you understand what to expect.

Generally, when you earn net self-employment income (net = income after all expenses) above $400 or so, you need to report that income and pay taxes on it. The tax is called "self-employment tax" and consists of Social Security and Medicare taxes. The percentage in 2017 is 15.3% on the first $127,200 in net self-employment income plus 2.9% on any net self-employment income above $127,200.

But that's not all; you also need to account for federal and state as well as possible local, county, and/or city income tax, which varies depending on your income. Again, in chapter 7 of this book, I will go into more details for tax as it is in the Liability chapter. For now, just know that you will need to withhold about 10% more for federal and state taxes.

Thus, in total, to prepare to pay your taxes, set aside at least 25% of your total self-employment income after expenses. If you earn $1,500 and subtract $500 for expenses set aside an additional 25% ($250) to pay your tax liability. Your net income after taxes is $750.

Income Planning For Life Events

Life is fun and exciting because it is full of surprises. Some are good, some are bad – and some we know are coming, but act surprised anyway. For the life events we know will happen, the more we can prepare for them financially, the better life will be for you when that event happens. These events might be marriage, having children, and old age that leads to illness, disability, and death. As you quickly realize, the older you become, the more life events happen, so I have a strategy to help you plan your income for life events. I call this the Root Income Strategy.

Sequoia Root Income Strategy (Science Based)[24]

To understand how I came up with this strategy is to first understand roots – tree roots. Specifically, the root system of the world's largest single tree and largest living thing by volume, Giant Sequoia trees. They are among the oldest living things on Earth. The oldest known giant sequoia based on ring count is 3,500 years old. These trees can grow to be about 30 feet in diameter and more than 250 feet tall.[25]

The rooting system of the Giant Sequoia during the first few years consists primarily of a taproot with few laterals. The taproot is the main root of a primary-root system that grows deep down to reach moisture and nutrients and provides structural stability. However, after 6 to 8 years, the deep elongation of the taproot practically stops, and lateral root growth takes over. Lateral roots grow outward and wide and can attach and cling to the soil, which makes them ideal for the prevention of erosion. This unique rooting habit is what makes the Giant Sequoia so different from every other plant and tree and what makes them the greatest tree.[26] Normally, plants and trees either have taproot or lateral root. Unlike all of them, the Giant Sequoia root system changes from taproot to lateral. It first goes deep and then goes wide.

When strategizing your income, imagine you are like the Giant Sequoia tree. First, focus on deepening your taproot, your one key income. Work hard and make sure that income "grows" deep enough to provide you with financial stability. Don't get distracted by other opportunities at this point, but focus on growing that taproot income. This income should generate a lot of cash so that you can increase your monthly net savings. Once your cash level reaches the amount necessary to invest your time into other income opportunities, then instead of working harder to "dig deeper" with that main income, work smarter and grow your lateral roots to build more income sources that can completely overtake the main income. This is "financial retirement," when the main root doesn't need to dig deeper for water and nutrients because its lateral roots have spread so wide that the tree gathers all it needs from them. Furthermore, by going wide with your "lateral root" income, you have increased your financial stability to withstand harsh conditions that others cannot withstand. Thus, similar to how the Giant Sequoia tree is the oldest living thing on Earth, you will not have to worry about outliving your income when you have Sequoia Income Roots generating your money. As you get older, your income roots will support your life growth and changes to weather all of life's elements.

Chapter Five
SAVING MONEY

"The habit of saving is itself an education. It fosters every virtue, teaches self-denial, cultivates the sense of order, trains to forethought, and so broadens the mind."-T.T. Munger

Income Statement		Balance Sheet	
Income	Expense	Assets	Liability
1. Income A	1. Expense 1	1. Asset A	1. Debt 1
2. Income B	2. Expense 2	2. Asset B	2. Debt 2
3. Income C	3. Expense 3	3. Asset C	3. Debt 3
Total Income: $ABC	Total Expense: $123	Total Asset: $ABC	Total Liability: $123
Company: Net Profit/Net Loss (Total Income-Total Expense) Net Profit: $		Company: Owner's Equity (Total Asset-Total Liability) Owner's Equity: $	
Individual: Net Savings/Net Burn (Total Income-Total Expense) Net Savings: $		Individual: Net Worth (Total Asset-Total Liability) Net Worth: $	

BUILDING ON CHAPTER 3 (DEVELOPING Your Money Smarts), this chapter is all about the Expense side of the income statement, giving you details and strategies for how to save money and increase your Net Savings. You will learn the key reason why people develop poor spending habits, strategies for saving money within each of the three specific types of expenses we discussed in Chapter 3 (fixed, variable, and discretionary expenses), and develop plans to save for key life events.

Logically, saving money is a "no-brainer." There is no need to dispute it or argue its importance. Saving money is the right and smart thing to do. But, people don't do it. In my quest to understand why I learned how neurologist Antonio Damasio discovered that decisions are made with emotions.[27] To summarize his findings, he studied people who had brain damage in the areas that control emotions. As it turned out, people who had brain injuries in those areas all had a very difficult time making decisions. His discovery suggests an answer to why people make bad decisions when they know they are wrong – emotions, not logic, drive them.

To add to this discovery, an experiment done by psychologist Dr. Walter Mischel at Stanford University shows that those who can control their emotions and delay gratification are more likely to succeed in life. This experiment is known as the marshmallow experiment.[28]

The marshmallow experiment asked a nursery school child (approximately four years old) to choose his favorite from among a tray of yummy treats containing marshmallows, cookies, and pretzels. After the child had chosen the treat he liked the most among the three options (let's say the child chose a marshmallow), the child was then given two trays to choose from. One tray had one marshmallow, and the other had two marshmallows. Which tray did the child choose? All children in the experiment chose the tray with the two treats.

At this point, the true experiment began. The examiner told the child that he/she could only have the tray with two treats if he were willing to wait until the examiner came back from "doing some work." The child was not given any idea of how long the examiner might be gone. The child could call back the examiner at any time by ringing a bell, but if they did so, they would only get the tray with one treat. The experiment required the child to wait for fifteen minutes before the examiner would return to the room to give the child the tray of treats.

Psychologist Dr. Walter Mischel has continued to study his original test subjects for the past 50 years, with shocking results. Overall, the preschoolers who were able to wait for two marshmallows all those years ago now as adults have a lower body mass index (BMI), lower rates of addiction, a lower divorce rate, and higher SAT scores.[29] Children who displayed self-control grew up to be adults who were able to conquer stress in pursuit of their goals and were "more able to sustain effort and deal with frustration," said Mischel.

For kids, it's sweet treats. For adults, it's self-treats. When you want it, you've got it. Everything is on-demand: on-demand TV, on-demand games, on-demand food, and on-demand transportation. Buy buttons are everywhere, on every device. Credit card, debit cards, and prepaid accounts are already set up.

You click, and it is shipped. 7 Days? Nope, too slow. 3 Days? Nope, not fast enough. Next Day? I now expect that... Same day shipping, within 2 hours? Now, I like that!

Self-control is required more than ever nowadays to save money in a world of free shipping, free returns, and "risk-free purchases." The "buy now and think about it later" mentality has led to adults racking up unmanageable credit card bills. Where is the self-control? Where is the delayed gratification? From instant noodles to instant messaging, it is hard to blame anyone for their lack of patience and self-control. However, those who have self-control and can delay gratification are certainly coming out ahead in this new world.

To help you save money, this section will discuss savings strategies specific to each type of expense: Fixed Expenses, Variable Expenses, and Discretionary Expenses.

Strategies to Save On Fixed Expenses

Fixed expenses are expenses that occur monthly at the same amount. Among fixed expenses, the most common are housing, car payments, insurance, and other fixed debt payments. Below I discuss the three common major fixed expenses and ideas for saving on them.

Housing

Housing is usually the biggest fixed expense both for renters and owners. Renters pay monthly rent, and owners pay a monthly mortgage payment to the bank. Mortgage is simply the money borrowed from a bank to buy a home, which requires the borrower to make monthly payments to pay back the loan. In Chapter 7 when I discuss liabilities in detail, you will learn more about mortgages.

To save money when you are renting, you must negotiate with the landlord or property owner. If you are a student living with your family, that's great for you but do give yourself the opportunity to be a financially responsible person and pay rent as well – no matter how much or little. It gives you self-respect and earns the respect of your family.

Negotiate the monthly rental price, who pays for water and electric, and who pays for ongoing major and minor maintenance. If you are struggling, there may be government housing programs, which I discussed earlier under benefit income in chapter 4, to assist you with paying rent. The biggest factor in your price is the type of rental. You should do your research to decide between renting part of a room that is shared with others, single room for yourself, studio, apartment unit, mobile home, manufactured house, townhome, condo, or single family house. Each varies in market price depending on the condition and area. The more research you do and the earlier you do it, the more options you have. If you find an area that you like with great pricing but no availability, leave your name and number with the property manager or owner and ask them to call you when something becomes available. As you visit each rental property to decide on which to rent, remember to control your emotions and practice self-control. If you have a bigger goal to save money so you can buy a house instead of renting, choose to delay your gratifications and wait to spend on things that you don't need. Just like the child who needed to wait for 15 minutes to get two marshmallows, wait to choose a lower priced rental unit. Don't give into instant gratification and sign a rental contract in a luxury place when it is not necessary and makes you unable to save more. While I understand the idea of living every day to the fullest, it also means I need to plan for my future days so that I can live those even fuller. I need to make certain preparations today. I choose to live today to the fullest within the plan I made for myself so that my future days are even more full, fun, and exciting.

When you have a family, the decision of where to live is even more emotional, because you want the best for your family all the time. Out of love and care, you might choose the decision to give them immediate gratification with a more expensive rental unit. But remember, that's only one marshmallow that the whole family has to share. When everyone waits, your family can actually own a dream home one day rather than renting forever. The key is honest communication and sharing the goal with them to save together as a family.

Growing up, my family was very open and honest about us not having money. So whenever I went grocery shopping as a child, other than what was needed for our family of eight to eat, I was told that we couldn't afford to buy the candy, toys, and impulse items that I wanted to get at the checkout counter. When my dad shared with me that he was only paid twenty-five cents to make a food delivery in which he sometimes needed to walk up many flights of stairs, it hurt me and would bring me to tears to think about spending that quarter during lunchtime at school on a bag of chips. So when my parents gave me money for school in the morning, I would go home and give it back to them. This included money to spend on school field trips, so I would just eat what my mom packed for me and drank water. It was painful to deny the ice cold beverages for sale on those hot sunny California days! Water did the job though, and coming home, I would give all the money back to my parents. My parents love me, and I love them, so that's how I showed my appreciation and my love back. The less money I spent, the less I knew they needed to work. It was the least that I could do for them, and I didn't feel a bit ashamed that my family didn't have a lot of money. In fact, it made me feel more mature than my friends to know that my parents told me the truth and enabled me to make money decisions. I am proud of my parents for who they are, and I appreciate their sacrifices, their humility, and their willingness to share with me how little they got paid and allow me to get involved with lowering the overall family expenses.

When my family looked for places to rent, it was clear from my parents that we just needed a roof, nothing fancy. The key was to save money so we would have money to live every day to the fullest and enjoy being with one another.

The way to save money when you own the house and pay a monthly mortgage payment to the bank is to refinance. Refinance describes the process in which a borrower restructures the mortgage loan to get a lower monthly mortgage payment. In Chapter 7, we will go into more detail about that process. But for now, just know that when it comes to lowering any fixed debt repayment loans, all you need is a phone call or meeting. Usually, you need to wait at least six months to a year before you can effectively renegotiate or restructure any fixed payment loan payments. Now that you know this before you commit to any monthly debt payments, ask them how often you can come back to renegotiate the payment. They should tell you how you can lower your payments and how often you can do it. You learn a lot and save a lot by asking this question.

After you read Chapter 7 to learn how to get a mortgage and calculate your monthly payments, you will be able to run an analysis to see if renting is more expensive than paying a mortgage. You might be surprised at how often this is the case! Renting can be more expensive than owning and paying a monthly mortgage. Continue reading, learning, and practicing so you can do this analysis for yourself and others. When you do, people will turn to you and say, "Wow you are so Money Smart!" At that point, you can give a very big smile. So big, your eyes squint like mine.

Car Payments

Car loans to me are the gateway debt for graduates. It is usually a graduate's first big financial monthly obligation that can lead to a bad level of comfort with gratifying now and paying for it over time. Certainly, the best savings strategy is to buy a car that you have the money to buy without borrowing and going into debt. If the car is bought in cash, there won't be any debt, period. By taking out a car loan and having monthly debt payments, you officially have to work for money. This is a path you certainly shouldn't want to take so willingly. No matter how little the payments are, it creates a long-term habit of taking on debt and spending future income. As a student who is supposed to focus on preparing for your career, having the debt payment distracts you. This small debt payment may cause you to choose work that is not beneficial for your career or limit your options, like taking a paying job instead of interning at a company that prepares you for your future. Other than car loan itself, which will be discussed more in detail in Chapter 7; I want to share with you a few strategies to get the lowest price for your car.

1) Research online.

Know the Manufacturer's Suggested Retail Price (MSRP) of the car before you go to buy it – information is power. MSRP is the full price, and the goal is to go below that as much as you can. My personal goal is 10% minimum below MSRP. Use car-pricing comparison apps and tools. I used the TrueCar tool, and it saved me money shopping in Southern California. I am sure there are other tools and resources to help you compare prices and research online.

2) Make an appointment with the right person.

Car dealerships have two types of car salespeople: commission salespeople and non-commission salespeople. When I buy my cars, I work with the non-commission salespeople. They are also known as the internet sales team or fleet sales team. Non-commission salespeople's performance measure is based on the volume of sales. They want to sell as much quantity or units as possible. Commission salespeople, as you already know, earn money based on their selling performance. Certainly, there are many great, honest, and helpful car salesmen who can give you even lower prices than the non-commission team because they are given more authority to adjust pricing. You just need to go through the experience and learn.

3) Come prepared.

Don't be a blank sheet of paper for the sales guy to write all over. Know how you plan on paying for the car. If you are not going to buy it with money you have, and need to borrow (which is called "financing" the car), understand your financing options before you go to the dealership. Visit a lender (like a bank) directly to discuss car financing instead of relying on the car dealership to be your bank. Outside banks and credit unions may offer much lower car financing rates, so know that before going to the dealership. If you already got financing from the dealership or had to use their financing for any reason, you still have the option to go to a bank or better, a credit union, to refinance it. Refinancing will be discussed in detail in Chapter 7. You just need to do it quickly as once your car is driven a certain number of miles (5,000 as a rule of thumb, but it depends on the bank), the car can be reclassified from new to used, and then the rates are higher. Don't wait − refinance it as soon as possible before your first bill comes.

4) Be confident. Knowledge is power so keep yourself up-to-date.

A great resource is to visit www.consumer.ftc.gov. Search for "vehicle financing" or "buying a car."[30]

5) Choose whether to lease or buy.

The car decision is similar to renting a house versus paying a mortgage. Once you learn more about loans in Chapter 7, you will be able to see that if you buy a car outright or with only a few years of auto loan payments (about three years or less); it generally saves you money over leasing.

Insurance Costs

The most common insurance costs for you are health, auto, property, and life insurance. I will discuss each so you have a better understanding of how you can save money and make the best decisions.

Health Insurance & Ways To Save On Health Care

The #1 cause of bankruptcy is medical bills.[31] While simply having health insurance isn't going to guarantee you to avoid medical debt, it is a wise investment to make because the risk is unimaginable without it. To help you save on your health insurance and health care cost in general, the following are some key ideas and practices:

1) Be healthy & safe

- Go back to the fundamentals of healthy living. Eat nutritious food, wash your hands, drink clean water, and exercise regularly. As the sayings go, "an ounce of prevention is worth a pound of cure." Choosing to live a healthy lifestyle is your best way to reduce and avoid health related costs.
- Follow and practice safety procedures. Accidents do happen so ensure safety practices to avoid major injuries.

2) Have regular checkups & be vaccinated

- Schedule your check up appointments. Most insurance plans cover regular checkups, so it will cost you nothing or very little. Many major health problems could have been treated easily and inexpensively if they were discovered early on.

- Get vaccinated when it is suggested by your medical professional. Often, they are offered freely or your insurance plan covers it. Take advantage of it.

3) Know what you need or are spending

- To save money, you first need to know what you are needing or spending. Insurance plans can be very different from each other. Choosing the lowest price health insurance plan may be the most expensive choice for you if you are not clear on what you need. If you are unclear of what you need, review your past year's activities and spending. Know how many times you visited the doctors, what medicine you bought, and other health services you spent money on. Review that information and see which insurance plan will save you the most.
- Consider key life events such as pregnancy and childbirth when selecting the appropriate insurance plan. Having the right insurance plan that will cover key needs during significant life events will save money and give you peace of mind.
- Increase your deductible to save monthly on your health insurance plan if you are young, healthy, and have a history of not needing to visit the doctor often. Likewise, do the opposite if the math works out better for you or family. The key is to track how you are using your health insurance.

4) Compare plans

- Invest the time to do your research and ask the professionals about all your available options. Learn about Health Savings Accounts (HSA), Preferred Provider Organization (PPO), Health Maintenance Organization (HMO), and Exclusive Provider Organization (EPO). Also, compare between private insurances and the Health Insurance Marketplace. I know you may not be familiar with them, but that's normal when starting out. Don't feel embarrassed by asking questions. In fact, most people don't know and just assume their way through it. You don't want to assume anything because ignorance is most expensive. Know that you have a lot of options so find the one that is most suitable for you by asking questions and doing research.

- Compare between employer group health plan options vs. individual plan options. Your family members may save by being a part of the employer group plan. There are requirements that need to be met, but it is worth the time to explore options that can save you money.
- Look for specialty plans for specific medical needs. Many health plans have specific benefits for certain health conditions like asthma or allergies. Don't be shy about asking them for how to best maximize their plan. For example, they may provide expensive equipment for you or give you options to buy it for lower than you would get it elsewhere.
- Ask for their complete list of benefits and take advantages of them. There are often benefits that are overlooked such as discounts on gym memberships, massages, fitness programs, and acupuncture.

5) Don't just accept whatever is billed or denial for coverage

- Take action when you notice mistakes or when you don't understand a billed amount. Various studies have found that medical bills are often incorrect. That can cost you money if you don't pay attention or aren't willing to ask for an explanation for numbers you don't understand. The cost for being too 'shy" or "afraid" or "lazy" to call can really cost you. The mistakes are honest mistakes, so they are very easy fixes when you let them know.
- Appeal the decision of your insurance to not cover your medical expense when it happens. There will be times when you understood the plan to cover a certain expense, and it got denied for coverage. When this happens, you can appeal the decision or be responsible for paying the medical bill. Don't feel you have to do this on your own. You can contact your state's insurance commission to help you with any disputes.

6) Avoid paying extra

- Know the medications you take and select the plan that covers it or provides discounts. Share your medication list to your insurance provider and doctor, so they know what's covered to help you save.

- Get referred without having to pay extra. When you need a specialist, let your doctor know your insurance plan details that include which specialist participates in your plan for the doctor to refer to. By doing this, your plan will be covering the cost for the specialist, so you don't have to be paying extra when it is referred to a specialist outside the plan's network.
- Go generic instead of brand name medications when a doctor approves. Well known brand names can be much more expensive than the generic brands of medications. Ask your doctor for generic brand recommendations to save money.

7) Work with the care provider to save money

- Discuss with your healthcare provider to save you money. For example, ask your dentist office to split the cost into two years and schedule the service accordingly so that the cost is spread over two insurance plan years.
- Ask your doctor if it is safe to split a higher-dosage pill in half to save cost since the higher-dosage pills and lower-dosage pills may cost you the same.
- Take the free sample size medicine from your doctor. Pharmaceutical companies give doctors free samples of medicines so ask your doctor if he might have the medicine you need.
- Kindly let your doctor, dentist, or other professional healthcare provider know you need to save money so they can work with you on alternative billing, treatments, and payment options that can save you money.
- Pay in cash for discounts. Find out if your healthcare provider will give you a discount if you pay in cash.
- Leverage low cost or free, convenient options using your healthcare provider online and telephone services. When your situation requires just questions and answers, you can save money and time by solving your need over the phone and online.

8) Know where not to go and where to go

- Always check before you make an appointment if the doctor or healthcare provider is part of your insurance plan coverage.

- Don't go to emergency rooms for non-emergency needs. The cost of emergency rooms is higher. If you are having some signs of illness, make an appointment before your illness becomes an emergency.
- Compare beforehand the cost of a local clinic and the cost of the emergency room. When you need urgent care, you will already know where to go for the least cost to you.

9) Find discounts and alternatives.

- Negotiate directly for lower prices. Most discounts are given when asked so just ask.
- Shop elsewhere. Your optometrist may have glasses for sale, but you may find that you can shop elsewhere for lower prices. Discuss the cost with both your health provider and your insurance plan to know your benefit options and costs.
- Consider using students or trainees to save. For example, instead of going to a dental office, visit a local dental school and ask for their service. You can save money while helping them gain experience.
- Understand first what treatments and procedures you need along with the cost before accepting it. Always ask if it is truly necessary and urgent. Discuss pricing, discounts, and alternatives up front.
- Take advantage of free offers. Often, communities will have health fairs that offer free health services. Take advantage of them.

10) Use a broker

- Leverage their knowledge to help you find the right plan for your needs. The key to having them effectively help you is to know what you need.
- Good brokers will first learn about your needs before making recommendations so don't be afraid to compare brokers as well. They will be the best people to answer your questions. Don't be afraid to ask. If they make you feel uncomfortable, find others. It is important that you have a good relationship with your broker, so they know how to solve your needs best while saving you money.

Saving Money On Auto Insurance

Auto insurance has options that can make a difference between you being in debt or not after an accident. With the options, the cost can vary, so the following are ways to save on auto insurance for you.

1) **Know what is required by your state and what minimum coverage you must maintain.**

You can easily find the minimum requirements on your state's website. Besides your state, if you finance the car, your bank may require a minimum amount of coverage.

2) **What you can afford isn't just what you can pay for the insurance but what you can't afford in case something bad happens.**

Many people go bankrupt when accidents happen (not just car accidents), and they do not carry enough insurance coverage. This usually relates to medical bills. Just think of the possibility: after an accident that knocks you unconscious, you wake up with a big medical bill that your insurance won't cover. Find out which of your insurance policies kick in after a car accident.

3) **Research and shop around.**

All insurance companies are different, so each will look at you as a risk differently. Each also has its own discount program. Use a comparison shopping tool to find the best rates.

4) **Review optional coverage that might be useful.**

If you don't have a backup car, getting rental car coverage is a good idea, and so is roadside assistance if you don't have access to help through another program. Consider "gap" coverage if it is offered, which covers the difference between the value of the vehicle and the amount owed on it. Gap insurance may even be required by your lender if you are financing because the loan may be worth more than the value of the car thanks to depreciation. Also, if you prefer original parts (OEM-original equipment manufacturing), you can select coverage for that, or else your insurance may only cover aftermarket or non-original parts when repairing your car.

5) Stop paying for coverage you may not need.

When you can afford to replace your car, and your car is paid off, review your premiums for collision and comprehensive. If the monthly premium is more than 10% of your car value, you may consider adjusting or decline that coverage altogether.

6) Know your deductible amount.

When you make an insurance claim, this is the amount of money you will pay. As an example, let's pretend that your car needs $1,500 of repairs, and you make an insurance claim to cover it. After all, that's a lot of money that you don't want to spend on repairs when you have been paying money for car insurance. Your insurance happily accepts the claim and then asks you to pay $1,000. Wait, huh? Then you find out that your policy has a $1,000 deductible. Since the repair costs $1,500 and the insurance pays for any amount above your deductible, they pay $500, and you pay $1,000.If the repair costs $1,000 or less, you will pay for all of it, so don't even bother calling your insurance if that is the case. Your car policy can have a deductible as low as zero, but lower deductibles are more expensive. It is all up to you. If you know that you are the type of person who would not bother calling your insurance company for small claims, you may just accept lower insurance costs with a higher deductible.

7) Maximize discount programs.

Almost every insurance company has discount programs, so ask for them. Here are some examples: package discounts when you buy car insurance with other insurance such as home or renters insurance, multi-car discounts, low mileage discounts, good student discount, good driver discounts, and discounts if you choose to pay in full instead of monthly. Finally, if you choose to pay by auto debt instead of credit card, you may be offered additional savings.

8) **Honesty is the best policy.**

If you lie on your insurance application to save money, your policy can be voided, and your claims denied.

9) **Keep your insurance company updated.**

If you have an agent, build a relationship with that person, as agents can be very helpful to you. When there are changes in your life, such as adding or removing a driver, buying a new car, or having a baby, let your insurance company and agent know as you may qualify for discount programs or promotions to save money.

Saving Money On Homeowners Insurance

When you own a home, besides the mortgage payment, you also need to have homeowners insurance, which is sometimes referred to as "property insurance." When you are a renter, you just buy renter's insurance, which you can ask your auto insurance company or agent to help you with as well. The bigger saving potential is in homeowners insurance over renter's insurance, so I will cover strategies specifically for this type of insurance.

1) **Compare prices locally and online**

- Ask your local insurance broker to help you while you compare your options online. Beyond the price comparison, compare the level of service you will get from the company you decide to work with.
- Get referred to the insurance company that your friends and family trust.
- Read the reviews of the different insurance companies to have an understanding for how they treat their customers when they do an insurance claim.

2) **Combine auto and home insurance**

- Give your current auto insurance company the opportunity to save you money by asking them if their insurance company also offer homeowners insurance. Often, they will be excited to increase their business with you and give you a bundle discount.

3) Increase your deductible

- Save money if you are the type of customer who will not call your insurance company for damages that you will try to fix yourself. By increasing your deductible, you will save money immediately. However, be prepared to have enough savings to cover the deductible amount when you do make an insurance claim. For example, if your deductible is $1,000, make sure to have that amount saved because that's what you will pay your insurance company first before they pay the rest of the cost for repair or replacement.

4) Know the accurate rebuilding cost for enough coverage

- As time changes, the cost to rebuild changes. Review your policy to keep this current. This is different from the market value of the property if you were to sell it. This would be the cost for the insurance company if they were to rebuild your house. When you don't have enough coverage, the insurance company will require you to pay the difference to rebuild.
- When you upgrade your property, the cost to rebuild will increase so update your policy when you upgrade.

5) Ask how you can lower your cost

- Increasing the security of the property can lower your insurance cost. This can be done by adding smoke detectors, home security systems, and other tools that reduce the risk of your house being burned, robbed or damaged.
- Seek discounts for seniors and other programs that you may qualify for.
- Maintain a good credit score and ask for discounts for being credit worthy.

6)   Update the value of your possessions

- Increase your coverage to protect additional personal possessions.
- Decrease your coverage as your personal possession depreciates in value. If you have assets that appreciate, you will then increase your coverage.

7)   Understand the liability risk and exposure you have

- Protect yourself from lawsuits. For example, homeowners insurance will cover liability resulting from visitors injuries in your property.
- Understand what your policy does and doesn't cover so you are aware of who to call when something happens on your property.

Saving Money On Life Insurance

Life insurance can cost you anywhere from dollars per day to hundreds per month. There are essentially two types of life insurance, pure life insurance and life insurance with cash value. The most affordable are pure life insurance, which is called "Term Insurance." The other type of insurance that has cash value has more options and more names. It is usually referred to as "Whole Life Insurance," "Universal Life Insurance," or "Variable Life Insurance." Below are a few ways to save on life insurance.

1)   Buy term insurance.

- Buy Term. Term life insurance is the most affordable and most popular. It is this pure life insurance that you buy for a set term of years with 10, 20, and 30-year policies the most common. Once the term is up, the coverage expires.

2)   Shop with an independent licensed insurance agent or broker

- Using independent agents allows you to access more insurance companies to find the best fit for your needs while saving you money. The key is to know what you need so they can be more effective at finding what's best for you. Since these agents are independent, they are not limited to any one insurance company.

- Go online and get quotes. An easy way to get an idea for how much you can save or expect to budget is to use online quoting tools. You can go directly onto insurance company websites and independent agency websites.
- The best way to save is to speak to an agent, so they can better understand your health condition and lifestyle to best direct you towards an insurance company that will look at you most favorably based on your answers.

3) Be upfront about your health conditions and lifestyle choices

- Save money and time by being honest. The most affordable options usually require a blood test and medical records so it is best to be upfront so you can get an accurate quote.

4) Buy when young and healthy

- Be proactive and get life insurance when you are young and healthy because the rates only go up as you age.
- Get approved before your health condition prevents you from getting any coverage.

5) Being healthy is the #1 way to save

- Lose weight and choose to practice a healthier lifestyle. Your insurance rate is based on your health so more healthy you are, the lower the cost.
- Don't smoke. Smokers pay much more for life insurance because they are considered higher risk.
- Quit smoking and request for qualification to lower your cost.

6) Avoid guaranteed issue (no medical exam) policies if you are healthy

- Do the full medical exams. There are policies for people who don't want to do a medical exam for various reasons that is more costly. When you are healthy, choose the options that save you the most money.

Insurance can be complicated so use a trusted licensed insurance professional.

Strategies to Save on Variable Expenses and Discretionary Expenses

Variable expenses occur monthly but at differing amounts. These expenses are mainly groceries, utilities, and transportation costs like gasoline and public transportation fares. The most dangerous variable expense is the variable minimum payment for credit cards. If you didn't read about this in Chapter 3, I recommend you turn back to that chapter and read it right now. It certainly gives you a very clear understanding of how a credit card keeps you in debt and how you can protect yourself from this trap.

Discretionary expenses are up to your decision making so they can vary monthly and vary in amount. In other words, it doesn't need to happen and when it does, how much you spend is up to you. Examples of these expenses are entertainment, shopping, gifts, and charitable giving.

Since both variable and discretionary expenses are up to you to control over the spending, the strategies to save may apply to both. In this section, I will cover key strategies and practices to help you increase your self-control and save money.

The ONE WORD that determines if you can save money or not is TRACKING.

Fixed expenses can be easily memorized as they occur every month at the same amount. You must track variable and discretionary expenses. Since you are tracking something already, track everything, including your fixed expenses so that you can get a full and accurate financial picture. Track, Track, Track. It is worth the emphasis as money is mostly now digitized, so you no longer see it or feel it being spent; you just swipe, click, and auto pay. If you don't track your money, you won't know where it is going.

1) Track.

This is the most powerful word in the world of saving money. If you ever want to know if you are actually saving money or not, or if another person is saving money or not, ask yourself or the person how you/they track expenses. Without an effective way to track your expenses, it is not possible to manage them. If you are wondering which way is the best way to track, I can tell you that the most common ways are to use software on a computer, apps on a mobile phone, or pen and paper. Depending on what form of money you use, your personality, and habits, you need to decide which method works best for you. The only important aspect is that you actually track. If you have a better way to track that is accurate and effective, then keep on doing that. Without tracking, no strategy will work. This is why I put it as #1 on the list of best practices.

2) Create a budget.

There are many ways to create your budget, but again, the key is that you find a budget that works for you as long as it hits the goal of saving money monthly. If you haven't created a budget yet, this is your guide. Start your budget with how much you want to save per month. Go straight to the point. In math, the closest distance between any two points is a straight line. Set how much you want to save first, and then set budgets for each expense type and categories within each of those expenses you learned here.

3) Separate accounts.

Create a separate account for your savings. Make this account hard to access, so it doesn't tempt you. Keep it at another banking institution, so it will be a hassle to get access to it. Set it up so that your budgeted savings amount gets transferred automatically so it is out of your sight and out of your mind. This will grow and grow and grow. When you read Chapter 6 about investing, you will then see how your savings provides the capital for investments that can make you truly wealthy.

4) Don't choke yourself in the process.

Naturally, we all need breathing room, a sense of freedom, and a reward system to keep us motivated to keep on doing what we are doing. Saving money takes more effort than spending it. Success is harder than failure. To keep your energy high and level of motivation up, one strategy is to set up a fun account for yourself.

Whatever is in that account, you can spend freely on anything. Have a small monthly budget that funds this fun account. Having this fun account makes tracking your money fun, as you see how much money is in your fun account along with the other numbers.

5) Eliminate any expenses that don't make sense.

For example, late payment fees, bank overdraft fees, cash advance fees, check cashing fees, traffic tickets, parking tickets, and a whole lot of "lazy" expenses that are caused by just being lazy. Think about these lazy expenses and train your mind to recognize and avoid them.

6) Use cash. Paying for things with cash hurts more.

In one survey, people who used cards spent two times as much as those who used cash. Emotionally, it is very hard to let go of the cash you have in your hand that you work so hard for. This is why casinos have you exchange your cash for chips to play. Similarly, this is also why arcades turn your cash into tokens to play with. By using cash, you will emotionally want to spend less.

7) Discuss big purchases

(examples could be $100 or more, or one day of work's worth of income) Discuss these purchases with another person who is not emotionally involved. By having to explain your purchase to another person who is not emotionally attached, it forces you to think logically about your decision.

8) Seek at least two alternatives to the purchase.

The first alternative is another way to get by without spending money at all. A second alternative is an option that costs less and serves the direct need.

9) Wait 24 hours.

Decisions made in haste create waste. Effective sales and marketing strategies attack your emotions to convince you to make quick decisions before logic can catch up to say no. Give yourself that time. Twenty-four hours is enough time to allow your logic to catch up with your emotion.

10) Review your cash & credit balances.

As we know, "the truth hurts." In this case, that hurt is a powerful way to remind you to spend on needs rather than wants. Review your balances at least monthly, but it is even better if you do it as often as possible that is most effective for you. Check your cash accounts as well as all your credit card balances to know how much debt you are in and how much you need to pay to each of them. Yes, see the expenses add up on your credit cards and the low cash balances. Let the hurt sink deep enough to drive behavioral change. The more you can help yourself control your emotions and delay your wants, the closer you are to financial freedom.

11) Get cash back if you are going to use credit cards.

Credit cards know that by getting more people to use their cards, they will make more money. One of the ways credit card companies compete for people to use their card is to offer cash back such as giving back 2% on all purchases. The trap is that they want you to use their card and make minimum payments. If you are going to use a credit card, you must have the cash to pay off the balance. In doing so, you will get 2% cash back so whatever cost you $100, is now only $98 because of the 2% cash back.

Ageless Money Saving Wisdom

Now that you have learned strategies and practices for saving money on each of the types of expense, I would like to share with you some Ageless Money Saving Wisdom that was passed on to me, and that applies to all types of spending.

Have Hope

Hope is a powerful force. Without this force, the greatest success stories would not be possible. Certainly, hope in itself isn't enough, but it is the key first step, followed by determination, hard work, and perseverance.

In a recent radio interview, a man shared the story of how he had lost his job, house, and girlfriend. He suddenly felt hopeless, and all he could focus on was surviving day by day. The future, in his mind, was only the present moment. Being hopeless, thinking about tomorrow was useless for him, so whatever he could get that day, he would live all day. Because he lost hope, he lost everything. Don't be like this man. Whatever happened has become history, don't relive it in the present and drag it into the future. There will always be people who have it better than you, but likewise, there will always be people who had it worse than you that became successful and inspiring. Don't compare yourself to those who have more and lose hope in yourself, but be grateful and prideful for what you have that others don't. Always have hope and believe. If you don't believe in yourself, nothing else matters. Saving money is for the future so you must believe in the future.

Have Purpose – The "Why Factor."

Know your "why factor" because that force picks you up when you fall, gives you the motivation to continue when you are defeated, and provides the energy that keeps you alive when you feel that you are going to die. Achieving your goals will not be a smooth journey as there will be good times and bad times. Similarly, saving money isn't going to be easy unless you have a deep "why factor" that can emotionally charge you and empower you to make the tough decisions.

The imagery of a deep "why factor" is a starving mother who does not eat to save food for her children, a father who works without rest to have extra money in case or family emergencies, and a student of a single parent who understands the love and sacrifices of the parent and works to become financially responsible.

Success is not what you achieve; it is who you become. It starts with being purposeful and starts at home. Saving is a personal matter so make it personal with your purpose.

Money Can Buy Happiness Too

Can money buy you happiness? Yes! Of course, it can. Try it for yourself by buying something that makes you happy, like ice cream on a hot, sunny day. However, while money can buy happiness, it certainly cannot buy ALL happiness. The greatest happiness is priceless but the ones with a price tag, usually the little pleasures or conveniences, you can certainly buy.

Vice versa, happiness can also buy money. Well, not directly, but it's a very big factor. Have you ever noticed people who are miserable at work and can't wait to leave? If you know people like this, you also know that many of them leave work and can't wait to spend the money they earned to buy them back their happiness.

Choosing to do what you love and to be happy with what you do not only saves you money but also gives you the greatest opportunity to be your best. Only when you are at your best can you can make the most money. Love is the limitless power that enables you to do the impossible.

Let Your "Wants" Drive You to Save

Fighting against your "wants" and only spending on what you "need" is hard, and I understand that. "Wants" are so much more fun and exciting to buy. They make you feel great. I have a strategy for you to stop fighting your wants and instead use that powerful force to help you save. Write out your wants and make them your savings goals. The more you want these goals, the more you will make it a priority to save. This way, you can first set aside the money from your income for your goals (big wants) and then spend what is left after savings. Don't make the mistake of saving what's left after spending but spend what's left after saving.

Without clear goals for why we need to save money, why bother? Remember, emotionally, we are being targeted by big corporations who spend millions to study our behaviors and emotions to manipulate or rather influence us into spending and buying their products and services. To combat such forces that drive you to spend, allow your goals to anchor you and prevent your money from drifting out of your pocket into the corporation's pocket.

It is natural for a person who works very hard to want to spend the money they earned as a form of reward or celebration. Nothing is wrong with that. However, instead of spending without goals, have your goals remind you of why you need to work so hard. You can't work this hard forever.

The size of your goal matters because if your goal is too small and easy to achieve, it will not be emotionally powerful enough to drive you to practice saving and over time develop the habit to auto save. The goal has to be big enough to challenge you. If it does not challenge you, it won't change you.

Have three different ranges of goals: short-term, medium-term, and long-term. Short-term goals should be smaller and allow you to build a rhythm and habit of saving and fulfillment. Achieving these short-term goals gives your mind the proof that it is working and the motivation and momentum to continue saving. Medium-term goals are bigger goals such as vacations that further excite you to save more and work harder. Long-term goals are big goals that anchor you to making smart spending decisions. The smarter the decision, the closer these long-term goals are. These big long-term goals might be to purchase your home, invest, retire early, live your dreams, and change the world. Without the big long-term goals, you will spend all your savings on your short and mid-range goals. Essentially, the short-term and medium-term goals simply create the habit and offer small self-rewards for saving so you can achieve your long-term goals. A big mistake people make is to not have long-term goals and to spend all their savings on short-term goals.

Once you set your goal, begin immediately to save for it. To build momentum, save whatever you can so you can see the savings increase. As your savings account balance increases, regardless of how fast, it builds excitement and energy. If you can, create a big visual on a wall in your house and mark how much money is saved towards your goal, like a thermometer. If you have a family, it gets everyone to participate and builds even more energy and excitement to save money.

As you practice saving for your goals, you are building your savings muscle just like the Olympic athletes who lift weights build their muscle. Think of these athletes when they were just starting out – they must have started with lighter weights with much repetition and increased the weight over time. What happens if a beginner goes straight to lifting the heaviest weight right away? Yikes! I wouldn't do it. The experience of failure can be so discouraging that the beginner might naturally avoid it and stop altogether. Saving money is also a muscle that needs building so save little by little based on your income and gradually increase as your muscle develops. This is how habits are formed, through practice. So practice and find ways to make saving money fun, just like children getting to eat their two marshmallows!

Chapter Six
INVESTING MONEY

"The secret to investing is to figure out the value of something and then pay a lot less."-Joel Greenblatt

		Balance Sheet	
Income Statement		**Assets**	Liability
Income	Expense	1. Asset A	1. Debt 1
1. Income A	1. Expense A	2. Asset B	2. Debt 2
2. Income B	2. Expense 2	3.`Asset C	3. Debt 3
3. Income C	3. Expense 3		
Total Income: $ABC	Total Expense: $123	Total Asset: **$ABC**	Total Liability: $123

Company: Net Profit/Net Loss (Total Income-Total Expense)
Net Profit: $

Company: Owner's Equity (Total Asset-Total Liability)
Owner's Equity: $

Individual: Net Savings/Net Burn (Total Income-Total Expense)
Net Savings: $

Individual: Net Worth (Total Asset-Total Liability)
Net Worth: $

THIS CHAPTER IS ALL ABOUT Assets. It covers investments that can build wealth for you. By now, you should have learned the two main objectives of investing, which are to produce income and create capital gains (Chapter 3) and get an overview for income producing investments (Chapter 4). This chapter is dedicated to teaching you about investing. The earlier you learn this, the better. Don't let fear cause you to do nothing until you can't do anything.

In this chapter, you will learn why having assets matters, the types of assets along with strategies and practices for each, and the tax implications of various investments.

Why Having Assets Matters

Having assets matters because Assets are Key to Building Wealth.

Fundamentally, the only way to have wealth is to own assets that appreciate in value and produce income. A person cannot work 24 hours a day, day after day, without tiring, but your assets can do that. So for anyone who wants to retire and have their assets produce money for them, investing is the vehicle. If a person is afraid of investing because he fears losing money, well he will lose money by default if he doesn't invest, thanks to inflation.

Inflation is the increase in cost which forces you to spend more money on the same purchases. For example, the prices of gasoline, food, and housing have consistently increased over the years. Although you might live on an income of $2,000 a month today, it doesn't mean you will be able to do so in 10 years. A good long-term estimate for the annual inflation rate is 3%. Using any available inflation calculator or compounding growth calculator, you will need $2,687.83 a month in 10 years to afford the same living cost of today's $2,000. Another way to understand this is that your money will lose value at the rate of 3% a year because the cost has increased, making your buying power less. This is why saving money is only the first step. If the money saved sits in an account without growing at least 3% per year, you are essentially losing money. Money must be invested in assets that can appreciate (grow in value) to outpace inflation.

By now, you should be familiar with the word appreciation, which describes the increase in the value of an asset. When an asset is sold at an appreciated value, the profit is called capital gains. What you don't want is for an asset to depreciate. Depreciation is the reduction of the value of an asset. For example, your car, phone, and electronics depreciate almost immediately when you buy it. To better understand this, think about buying "open box" items or "returned" items at stores. You do not pay full price as the item is no longer in mint condition. Likewise, when someone wants to sell you an item that is used or pre-owned, they cannot sell the item to you at the price they paid for it. They will get less because the item has depreciated. The buyer saves a lot of money buying used items that have already depreciated because the seller absorbed the loss. This is why most rich people who understand depreciation do not buy new cars but rather buy used cars. They prefer other people absorb the loss of depreciation and not them. Similarly, rich people spend money on things that appreciate in value. In such a case, it is no longer considered spending, but investing. Spending is buying something that depreciates. Investing is buying something that appreciates in value.

Owning assets that appreciate in value rather than spending on things that depreciate is what separates the rich and the poor regarding financial net worth. In the chart below, you can see the sad reality of how much wealth is owned by the top 20% versus the remaining 80% of the US population.[32]

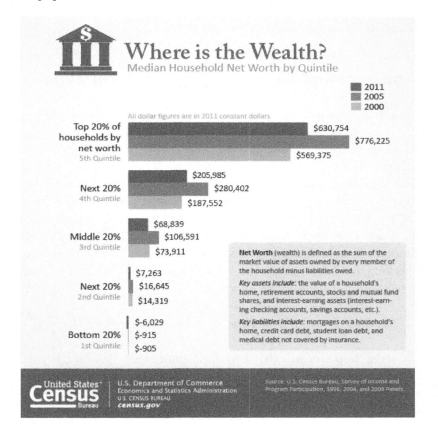

Key Point of The Data
  • The top 20% is worth more than twice the combined median net worth of the 80%

The fundamental difference between the top 20% and the others is that they control their spending on things that depreciate and invest in things that appreciate in value. Financial net worth is calculated by adding total asset value and subtracting any liabilities (debts). The more the assets appreciate in value, the greater the total asset value, which increases net worth. Having assets, specifically appreciating assets, is key to building your wealth.

If owning assets is the key to building wealth, which assets should you invest in? There are many assets, but to guide your understanding, I have grouped them into seven categories: Cash Accounts, Retirement Accounts, Lifestyle Assets, Real Estate Investments, Business Investments, Intangible Assets, and Market Investments.

Strategies and Practices for Each Asset Type

Cash Accounts

Cash Account is any account that holds your money. These include bank accounts that are usually your checking and savings account; online accounts that include online banks and PayPal; and other type of accounts that include store credit accounts, gift cards, and cryptocurrencies such as Bitcoin and Ethereum. When choosing which bank, which account, and other forms of cash to use, do your research and seek advice from a financial professional. Below, I will cover Checking and Savings Accounts as you most likely use these and can benefit from further understanding.

Savings Account(s) & Interest Checking Account(s).

These accounts are offered by banks and credit unions. They are FDIC insured up to $250,000. You can visit any local bank and open a savings account. Checking accounts may not pay interest, but if you shop around, you can find ones that do. Savings accounts generally give you relatively low return on your investment per year. It fluctuates, so ask before you open, and shop around different banks and credit unions. While the interest is low, a savings account does have specific benefits for you.

- **Liquidity:** It is easily accessible without any lock-up. Some other accounts may offer higher interest rates but require you not to withdraw your money for a set period of time.

- **Emergencies:** Life is interesting because it is unpredictable. You may have bad days and possibly even bad months of no income. During the economic downturn in 2008, many people lost their jobs and investment money when the stock market crashed. Worst, many of those people struggled because they didn't have any emergency money. As a best practice, you should have at least six months of emergency money, so you have adequate time to turn your financial life around.

- **Good Habit:** A savings account becomes your holding account for the money you save monthly. Saving monthly is a practice that builds a good habit. As the balance grows monthly, it becomes an exciting motivator for you to continue the habit until it becomes a lifestyle. As a result, you will become a better money manager and make smarter spending decisions, and when you become a parent, you will set a good example for your kids.

- **Strategic Accounts.** Remember from our discussion about saving money that you can open more than one of these Savings Accounts and set up one of them to be your "Fun Account" and another to be your "Capital Investment Fund," which is money specifically set aside for investing.

Other Cash Accounts

The key practice is to understand how safe it is to have your money stored in an account if it is not FDIC insured and to make sure to keep close track of it. For example, too often, we don't keep track of gift cards, and according to a study in 2017, one billion dollars of gift cards go unused each year.[33] As for highly volatile cryptocurrencies like Bitcoin and Ethereum, understand that these are high risk and consider asking the advice of a professional before storing your cash in one.

Retirement Accounts

The three most common retirement accounts are 401(k), Individual Retirement Accounts (IRAs) and Pension Plans. The one other way to save for retirement will be using cash value life insurance policies.

401(k) Plans

While many employers offer 401(k) plan benefits, many workers don't fully understand them to take advantage of the benefits. To introduce you to this, first know that a 401(k) is not an investment itself but rather an account that contains investments for its participants to choose from. The investment options to choose can range from a few options to hundreds. These investments are generally "market investments" that are later discussed in this chapter. The main point is that the choice should be made with the help of a financial planner who can help you understand each option and suitability for your age and risk tolerance.

What makes 401(k) plans attractive to workers is that the employers can contribute money into the account (think of free money from employers) and the money the worker put into the account is not going to be taxed until it is withdrawn.

The employer contribution is usually referred to as "401(k) matching" and generally matches up to 3% to 6% of the worker's pay. What "matching" means is that the worker must first participate in putting money into the account and then the employer will match the amount up to a certain set percentage of the worker's pay. For example, when an employer matches up to 5% (dollar for dollar) of the worker's pay and the worker is paid $100,000 per year, the worker can potentially get up to an extra $5,000 per year in their 401(k) account. If the worker puts in $3,000 over the year, the employer will match the $3,000 over the year, so the total will be doubled in the account. However, if the worker puts in $6,000, the employer will only put in the max amount of $5,000, so the total account value will be $11,000. This is why it is a best practice for workers to put money into their 401(k) that maxes out the employer matching. It is an immediate 100% return on your investment. It is important to discuss the details with your employer. Some employers will match dollar for dollar while others will match a percentage of your contributions (for example, 50 cents for every dollar you put in) up to their set limit amounts.

401(k) plan is often referred to as a "qualified" plan. "Qualified' plan can simply mean a plan in which the money that is contributed into the plan will not be taxed until it is taken out. The advantage of having the money not be taxed until it is withdrawn is to allow the money grow tax-deferred. The way that workers have their money contribute to their 401(k) is by deducting a portion of their paycheck. In the example when an employer matches 5%, the worker may set to have 5% of their paycheck be deducted to be put into their 401(k) to maximize the employer matching program. This deduction in a paycheck will reduce the taxable income amount so the worker can save on tax.

The United States Internal Revenue Service (IRS) sets pre-tax contribution limits so it can change from year to year. In 2017, the limit was $18,000 for workers under age 50 and $24,000 for people age 50 or older[34]. This limit amount only applies to the worker's contribution amount and will not calculate the employer matching amount.

One of the main reasons why employers have 401(k) plan benefits is to retain good people. Employers can do this by requiring the employee to work for a minimum amount of years before the company match vests. The term "vest" means that the employee fully earns the right to the money in which if he leaves the company, he can take that money with him.

When an employee leaves a company, the 401(k) amount can be moved to another qualified plan. This term is called a "401(k) rollover." If the employee decides to withdraw the money, the money will be both subject to income tax and a 10% early withdrawal penalty. To avoid withdrawal penalties, the employee must wait until he reaches 59-½ years old.

Rolling over to another qualified plan can mean having the account transfer to the new employer's qualified plan or into an Individual Retirement Account (IRA).

Individual Retirement Accounts (IRAs)

Unlike 401(k), which are accounts provided by employers; IRAs are accounts which can be opened by the person. This can be done by visiting a financial institution such as banks.

IRAs are similar to 401(k) in that it is not an investment itself but an account that holds a person's investments. There are two main IRAs. Traditional and Roth IRA. Both types allow you to save money for retirement with special tax treatments however each will have different advantages and regulations. This chart highlights some of their similarities and differences.[35]

Features	Traditional IRA	Roth IRA
Who can contribute?	You can contribute if you (or your spouse if filing jointly) have taxable compensation but not after you are age 70½ or older.	You can contribute at any age if you (or your spouse if filing jointly) have taxable compensation and your modified adjusted gross income is below certain amounts (see 2016 and 2017 limits).
Are my contributions deductible?	You can deduct your contributions if you qualify.	Your contributions aren't deductible.
How much can I contribute?	The most you can contribute to all of your traditional and Roth IRAs is the smaller of: $5,500 (for 2015-2017), or $6,500 if you're age 50 or older by the end of the year; or your taxable compensation for the year.	
What is the deadline to make contributions?	Your tax return filing deadline (not including extensions). For example, you can make 2016 IRA contributions until April 18, 2017.	
When can I withdraw money?	You can withdraw money anytime.	
Do I have to take required minimum distributions?	You must start taking distributions by April 1 following the year in which you turn age 70½ and by December 31 of later years.	Not required if you are the original owner.
Are my withdrawals and distributions taxable?	Any deductible contributions and earnings you withdraw or that are distributed from your traditional IRA are taxable. Also, if you are under age 59 ½ you may have to pay an additional 10% tax for early withdrawals unless you qualify for an exception.	None if it's a qualified distribution (or withdrawal that is a qualified distribution). Otherwise, part of the distribution or withdrawal may be taxable. If you are under age 59 ½, you may also have to pay an additional 10% tax for early withdrawals unless you qualify for an exception.

Pension Plans

Employers have another way to retain and recruit good people by offering pension plans to their employees. The advantage for employees is that Pension Plans require the employer to contribute the money and employees may or may not be required to contribute to the pension plan. The pension plan typically guarantees the employee a certain amount upon the employee's retirement. What the guarantee means is that the employer takes the risk of meeting the future financial obligation to provide retirement income for their retired employees. To qualify, the employees will need to meet the employer's set requirements such as length of employment.

Cash Value Life Insurance

Other than the common retirement account such as 401(k), IRAs, and Pension Plans, another option to save for retirement is to use a cash value life insurance policy. Introduced in Chapter 5, term life insurance only pays a death benefit, but when you choose to buy cash value policies like whole life, universal life, and variable life insurance policies, these policies can act as your retirement accounts in addition to providing a death benefit. To ensure suitability and understand the pros and cons for your situation using this option, please consult and work with a licensed insurance professional or other financial professionals such as your certified financial planner.

First and foremost, invest in a cash value policy if you have a need for life insurance. Then consider adding money to the monthly premium to build the cash value that is invested to save more for retirement. I'll quickly review the main needs for life insurance:

- Replacing income for your dependents. This can be your spouse, children, and other key people in your life. The life insurance benefit should be enough to sustain the current lifestyle of your dependents when you are not there to provide for them. This is what it means to replace your income.
- Planning for estate taxes if you have large estate taxes upon your death.

Key information and strategies for using cash value life insurance as a retirement tool include:

- It is not common, but your insurance premiums MAY be tax deductible. This depends on if your employer offers the option to purchase life insurance through the company's qualified retirement plan or not. If so, it may be possible to have your premiums be tax deductible within limits. Work with a qualified licensed insurance agent to help you with the details.
- Your cash value investment grows tax deferred. This means that the cash value portion of the policy grows without being taxed until you begin to withdraw the funds or surrender the policy.
- You can withdraw the cash from your cash value amount. Different policies will have different rules and fees associated. Before you make a withdrawal, consult your licensed agent or read your plan document to learn about the details.
- You can borrow against your cash value. The cash value balance in your insurance policy acts as collateral for your loan. A possible reason to take a loan from your cash value is that insurance policy loans are generally not taxable (though there are exceptions). Withdrawals are taxable. Upon your death, your loan would be paid off by your death benefit.
- Death benefits paid to beneficiaries are not subject to federal income tax with few exceptions. One exception is if the insurance was sold, which subjects the death benefit to the transfer-for-value rule. The other exception is when the cash value life insurance is held in a qualified retirement plan. Policies and rules are many and can be confusing so work with a licensed agent to help you before making any decisions.

Lifestyle Assets

I quickly mentioned these assets in Chapter 3.These are assets that support your lifestyle, like your car, clothes, shoes, and house. I specifically group these assets together because these are personal assets that generally depreciate in value (with the exception of your house). The biggest depreciating asset in this group is your car.

The main strategy for Lifestyle Assets is to delay living the lifestyle of the rich until you are truly rich. What I mean is, increase your lifestyle to live more like the "rich" when you have assets making enough money cover all your expenses with extra to support your "rich" lifestyle. While in the process of becoming "rich," choose a lifestyle that increases your Monthly Net Savings so you can more quickly become rich and STAY rich.

Real Estate Investments

Investing in real estate is very popular because not only does this investment produce income (as you were made aware of in Chapter 4) with rentals but it can also be sold for capital gains when the price appreciates higher than the purchase price. In addition, real estate gives the investor tax benefits such as deducting the mortgage interest to lower income tax owed, which will be covered in Chapter 7.

Real estate investments can be made creatively so I will share with you the main strategies to be aware of. You can further explore these when you are ready to invest. These strategies are: Buy and Rent, Buy and Sell (flip), and Other.

Buy and Rent

When using the Buy and Rent strategy, there are many types of real estate to buy and many ways to rent. Here are some of the most common:

- Buy land and rent it. Remember how I said real estate could be creative? In 1898, China leased Hong Kong and its surrounding islands to Britain on a 99-year lease. Thus, in 1997, Britain transferred control back to China. How is that for renting land! I share this, so you think as big and as creatively as you can, just as long as you can get a renter to agree to rent. The common ways are to rent the land for commercial development, mobile home parks, or car parking. Other creative strategies are to have billboard advertising and cell phone towers on your land.
- Buy mobile homes (manufactured homes), townhomes, condominiums, single family houses, duplexes (2 family unit property), and triplexes (3 family unit property) and rent the entire house or individual family units. This is very common, and you can set month-to-month rentals with higher rental

prices or lower prices with longer-term rental contracts (one year or more). Nowadays, the option to rent daily through services like Airbnb has further increased total potential rent revenue.

- Buy a house and rent the rooms. Instead of renting the entire house to a single renter, you can increase your total rent by renting individual rooms. This is common for real estate property near colleges.
- Buy fourplexes (multi family residential building with four units) or apartments and rent out the units. With four or more units, a building is now considered a commercial property. As a commercial property, the commercial mortgage loan will have different requirements than the residential mortgages. This will be covered in Chapter 8, Liabilities.
- Buy buildings and rent them out to businesses. The strategy to increase rental income from commercial buildings is to change the type of businesses you rent to. For example, restaurants generally pay higher rental prices than retailers.

Buy and Sell (Flip)

When using the Buy and Sell (Flip) strategy, the key is to buy the property at a low price so you can sell it for maximum profit (capital gains). Do expect to fix these types of properties up, which may take longer than you originally estimated. If you can sell during the hot-selling summer months when kids are out of school and moving a family is easiest, the prices will be on the higher side due to increased demand. Furthermore, having access to trustworthy contractors who specialize in "fix and flip" will give you great prices to increase profit. The key is still to buy low, so here are strategies to buy low so you can sell high:

- Buy real estate at an auction. Research is a must so before bidding, do your due diligences. The last thing you want is to win something you will lose money on. Auction properties are usually sold by lenders (banks) who foreclosed on the property, meaning they took it back from owners who could not continue making the mortgage payments.
- Buy real estate that is bank-owned. These properties are called Real estate owned (REO). When banks cannot sell a property at

auction or prefer not to use an auction, this property goes to the public for sale through real estate agents that handle REOs. It is a good idea to have relationships with these agents as they can give you great access to properties that can be profitable for you.

- Buy short sales. This happens when the owner sells the property below the mortgage amount owed to the lender. It is called short because it is short of meeting the amount needed to pay the current mortgage balance. For this to happen, short sales must be approved and accepted by the mortgage lender, who agrees to take less than what they are owed.

- Buy the ugliest house on the block. Because it is the ugliest house in the neighborhood, it has great potential to get fixed up and be worth more after it is beautified. The key is how you do your analysis of "beautification" and how fast you can do it to sell it during the best months of the year.

- Buy pre-construction. When developers build big projects, they may sell earlier units at a discount to raise cash to fund their development. When you buy these, you can wait until the full project is completed and sell the unit at the new higher price for capital gains.

- Buy a house with potential to build. If the house has a big lot of land that can be built upon with local government permits, it can earn a nice profit. You need to do a deep analysis of cost, timing, and construction teams.

- Buy a house from a motivated seller. Just like buying anything, if the seller is more motivated than the buyer, the buyer can negotiate a lower price.

- Buy houses in bulk. There are occasional opportunities to buy a "portfolio" of REO from banks or other lenders. These are not common, but I want you to be aware of the possibilities.

Other

There are other real estate investments besides buying to rent or sell. The following are some others strategies:

- Buy land and build. This is you becoming a developer. Certainly, this strategy requires specific knowledge and skills. The profit potential is huge when you can do this.

- Buy Real Estate Tax Liens. This is when you pay the local government property taxes owed by the owners of real estate who didn't pay in exchange for interest payments from the property owner, with the possibility of getting the property itself if the owner does not make timely payments to you. Since this is on the local government level, do your research with a city official.

Business Investments

The next type of investment is building and developing businesses. In Chapter 4, I introduced the 5Ps of Business Development (People, Positioning, Product, Promotion, and Profits) to use when you are building your own business for income. Here, I will discuss selling your business to produce capital gains and how investors can increase your business value. Furthermore, I will guide you on your business plan and business feasibility.

Strategic Practices for Selling Your Business

Prepare. Give yourself at least one year to prepare your financials, which should include at least three years of tax returns, with your financial professional. Prepare documentation for business operations so the new owner can have a smooth transition assuming ownership. This will allow potential buyers to have a better experience reviewing your business financial records and overall confidence in the business operation. Also, plan that it will take from six months to two years on average to sell your business. Don't pull back from the business in the interim because it might hurt your business and its overall value to potential buyers.

Get It Appraised. So you know the value of the business, hire a professional to calculate an appraised value. Keep in mind; the price is heavily dependent on the specific factors that the buyer values. I have seen businesses with $3 million in revenue sold for over $30 million dollars and others for $1 million or less. The range is large, and therefore a professional appraiser can give you a good reference point. Your business may not have any revenue at all but may contain other valuable features. You need to do your research to learn how similar companies to yours are valued and sold.

Sell your business on your own or hire a broker. You can save money by selling on your own or negotiate a fair broker fee to have someone do it for you.

Getting Investors to Increase Your Business Value

Instead of selling your business completely, another option is only to sell fractions. Another way to understand this is to allow investors to invest into your business in exchange for an ownership stake. To help you understand, I'll give you a historical example.

In June 2006, Yahoo wanted to buy Facebook for approximately $1 billion.[36] Facebook at that time was only two years old, and founder Mark Zuckerberg was 22 years old. Facebook only had around eight to nine million users and $20 million in revenue. $1 billion seemed like a nice pay day. However, Mark Zuckerberg turned Yahoo down.

A year later, Facebook sold a 1.6 percent ownership stake to Microsoft for $240 million. This immediately gave Facebook a value of $15 billion.[37] The decision to wait one year and accept the offer from Microsoft increased the business value from $1 to $15 billion.

When you legally start a business entity such as a corporation, you can determine how many shares your company will have. Certainly, it will be all owned by you. When anyone else is interested in investing in your company, you can then sell them parts of your ownership stake. Privately, you and the investor decide how much money the investor puts in and how much ownership you will exchange for that amount of money. That is essentially how private equity investment works.

In May 2012, Facebook opened its doors to public ownership by making its stock available on public exchanges, which turned Facebook from a privately held company into a "public company." The term for offering stock to the public for the first time is Initial Public Offering (IPO). On May 12, 2012, Facebook offered 15% of its company shares to the public. The remaining 85% continued to be held by the owners, who included the founder Mark Zuckerberg and other early private investors. To offer 15% of the company to the public, investment bankers had to figure out how to price each share for the public to buy. It was eventually agreed to offer 421 million shares at $38 each, giving Facebook a value of $104 billion dollars.[38] If the public decided to buy each share for less, Facebook's overall value would go down, and vice versa. After the initial price of $38 had started moving based on market demand, Facebook was valued in part based on the stock price. This why the company is now considered "public" because the public now owns part of the company. The price of the share is governed by supply and demand of the people.

On the morning of Facebook's IPO, CNBC reported "some 82 million shares were traded in the first 30 seconds. Seven minutes after the opening, 110 million shares had traded, with the stock eventually reaching a high of $45 a share. By 3:30 pm EDT Friday, Facebook volume—shares traded—set the record by exceeding General Motors' 458 million shares on its first day of trading. As trading went back and forth, so did the price. Less than 20 minutes after the opening, prices fell below $39. It did reach a high of $45 a share. As of 12:43 p.m. EDT, nearly 300 million shares had traded. At the market close of 4 p.m. EDT, the price was listed as $38.23. The total volume of 573,622,571 shares was exchanged."[39] Facebook was worth 104 billion dollars at the end of its first day of trading.

What did that mean for the founder of Facebook? As the creator, he had 28.2% ownership of Facebook after selling stakes to various private equity investors before going public.[40] At 28.2% ownership, he had the equivalent of 463 million shares, and on the day of the IPO, he sold 30.2 million shares to receive over $1 billion in cash while keeping 443 million shares, worth $16.9 billion at $38 a share price.[41]

This is how investing in building your own business can make you a millionaire and even billionaire.

Creating a Business Plan

I was told that "failing to plan is planning to fail," so having a business plan is an important step in helping your business succeed. This plan is what investors want to review before they invest so the better your plan is, the better investors can make decisions to invest in your business. Below, you will learn the key parts of a business plan in question format to serve as a guide as you develop yours. My knowledge of this came from my USC professors who are instrumental to my success.

1) What pain or problem do you or your business solve?

- I was taught by my USC entrepreneurial professors that businesses simply solve pains for profits. Thus, the bigger the pain or problem you solve, the bigger the business opportunity.

2) How is your solution (business) unique? How does it give you an unfair advantage in the marketplace?

- For you to successfully compete directly with competitors or indirectly with alternative solutions, having a unique selling proposition will be critical for your customers to choose your solution. You need unfair advantages that set your solution above the others to increase your business positioning.

3) Who is your target customer?

- A business becomes a business when it has a paying customer. It's important to understand the difference between customers and consumers. Your customers pay you while consumers are the users who benefit from your products and services. For example, your business creates baby toys. Your target customers are the baby's parents while your consumers are the babies.

4) How will you reach your target customers?

- Based on your target customers, you must research where and how they can be reached to create your marketing campaigns. Your marketing cost can either be fixed or variable.

5) What is your revenue model?

- This is about how your business makes money. Is your business going to be a recurring sales business where your customers can repeat business with you or no? Will your solution be offered for free with premium paid options, as is common with mobile applications? Does your revenue come from giving advertisers access to your users? Your business can have multiple different revenue models but should have strategies specific to that revenue model to execute.

6) Why you?

- Investors invest in the person more than they invest in the actual business. What makes you qualified to build this business? This is where your knowledge, experience, skills, and character shine.

7) Who's on your team?

- Teams can make the biggest dreams come true. It doesn't matter how big, wild, or "impossible" your business plan is, when you can share it with a team, it can make believers out of people.

Business Feasibility Study

What separates a great business plan from just a good one is a business feasibility study. The purpose of having this study is to prevent waste of capital that you could have invested into building the business. While this process can be extensive, below are some of the key aspects to consider:

1) Product or Service

- Provide supporting evidence of the quality, uniqueness, and need of your solution.

2) Market Environment

- Provide research on the size of the overall business opportunity for your solution and the potential demand for it. Identify the influential players and forces in the market for your solution. Gather key factors such as demographic, psychological, and behavioral information that supports your target customer buying your solution. Include data that supports your business model. How is it similar or different from other proven models?

3) Sales & Marketing

- Will your business have any strategic partnerships or market access? How will your pricing support your sales and marketing strategy? Will you need to offer payment terms to your customers? How will your customers buy?

4) Logistics & Operations

- Provide details for how you will secure your products or the facility to provide your services. Will your staffing and operations include outsourcing and sub-contracting?

5) Intangible Assets

- Is there any intellectual property that is used, and if so, how it is protected? Does the business need to license for other intellectual properties to operate?

6) Legal Considerations

- Provide how your business will comply with and stay within any pertinent legal regulations.
- What licenses will it need to operate and how and when will those required licenses and credentials be obtained?

7) Risk Assessments

- Present Porter's Five Forces Analysis. The five forces are the threat of new entrants, threat of substitutes, bargaining power of customers, bargaining power of suppliers, and industry rivalry.[42]
- Present PEST Analysis: Political, Economic, Social and Technological factors.[43]
- Present SWOT Analysis: Strengths, Weakness, Opportunities, and Threats.[44]

8) Timing

- Provide considerations that support the timing of your business launch.

9) Financial Projections

- Provide financial projection statements that include: Income Projections, Balance Sheet Projections, Cash Flow Projections, Break-Even Analysis, and Startup Cost Analysis.

Intangible Assets

Intangible assets are assets which are not physical in nature. Examples of these are patents (i.e. inventions), trademarks (i.e. brand name), copyrights (i.e. authorship), licenses (i.e. distribution rights), and goodwill. Among all types of assets, intangible assets can be the most valuable of all. For example, when Yahoo purchased Tumblr for about $1 billion dollars, $751 million was for intangible "goodwill" value; Tumblr's intangible assets represented 75% of its sale price.[45]

What does this mean for you? Your most valuable asset is you – your intangible personal development value. The more you invest in your own personal development, the more valuable you become. Your knowledge, experiences, skills, and character – you – are priceless. In fact, the more you fail the more valuable you become because you learn more from your failures than your successes. What that means is that when you fail or lose money, this experience goes into your intangible asset account and makes you more valuable. Certainly, your schooling cost, academic degrees from college, and professional certifications and designations go into this asset account. Remember, who you are is most valuable and irreplaceable. The best investment you can ever make is an investment in you.

Market Investments

Investing in the markets can be very confusing with so many options and risk levels. The single best strategy is to work with professionals who have the right credentials. Below, I will share with you the key professionals and credentials so you can choose the best for yourself. Next, you will learn the common types of market investments.

The Professionals, Firms, and the Credentials to Consider

- **CFP:**[46] A Certified Financial Planner (CFP) refers to the certification owned and awarded by the Certified Financial

Planner Board of Standards, Inc. The CFP designation is awarded to individuals who successfully complete the CFP Board's initial and ongoing certification requirements. Individuals desiring to become a CFP professional must take extensive exams in the areas of financial planning, taxes, insurance, estate planning, and retirement.

- **CFA:**[47] The Chartered Financial Analyst (CFA) is a professional designation given by the CFA Institute that measures the competence and integrity of financial analysts. Candidates are required to pass three levels of exams covering areas such as accounting, economics, ethics, money management, and security analysis.

- **ChFC:**[48] The Chartered Financial Consultant (ChFC) is a professional designation that denotes completion of comprehensive courses in financial education, examinations, and practical experience. Chartered Financial Consultant designations are granted by the American College upon completion of seven required courses and two elective courses. Those who earn the designation are understood to be knowledgeable in financial matters and have the ability to provide sound advice.

- **CLU:**[49] The Chartered Life Underwriter (CLU) is a professional designation for individuals who wish to specialize in life insurance and estate planning. Individuals must complete five core courses and three elective courses and successfully pass eight two-hour, 100-question examinations in order to receive the designation.

- **RIA:**[50] A Registered Investment Advisor (RIA) is an advisor or firm engaged in the investment advisory business and registered either with the Securities and Exchange Commission (SEC) or state securities authorities. RIAs have a fiduciary duty to their clients, which means they have a fundamental obligation to provide suitable investment advice and always act in their clients' best interests.

Types of Market Investments to Consider & Discuss With Your Financial Professional

Below are common market investments. Each carries its own level of risk, so it is best to work with a trusted financial professional. To help you become familiar with the details for these market investments

I used Investor.gov. Investor.gov is your online resource to help you make sound investment decisions and avoid fraud brought to you by the SEC's Office of Investor Education and Advocacy.

Stocks[51]

Stocks are a type of security that give stockholders a share of ownership in a company. Stocks also are called "equities."

Why Do People Buy Stocks?

Investors buy stocks for various reasons. Here are some of them:

- Capital appreciation, which occurs when a stock rises in price
- Dividend payments, which come when the company distributes some of its earnings to stockholders
- Ability to vote shares and influence the company

Why Do Companies Issue Stock?

Companies issue stock to raise money for various things, which may include:

- Paying off debt
- Launching new products
- Expanding into new markets or regions
- Enlarging facilities or building new ones

What Kinds Of Stocks Are There?

There are two main kinds of stocks, common stock and preferred stock.

- Common stock entitles owners to vote at shareholder meetings and receive dividends.
- Preferred stockholders usually don't have voting rights, but they receive dividend payments before common stockholders do and have priority over common stockholders if the company goes bankrupt and its assets are liquidated.

Common and preferred stocks may fall into one or more of the following categories:

1) Growth stocks have earnings growing at a faster rate than the market average. They rarely pay dividends and investors buy them in the hope of capital appreciation. A technology startup company is likely to be a growth stock.

2) Income stocks pay dividends consistently. Investors buy them for the income they generate. An established utility company is likely to be an income stock.

3) Value stocks have a low price-to-earnings (P/E) ratio, meaning they are cheaper to buy than stocks with a higher P/E. People buy value stocks in the hope that the market has overreacted and that the stock's price will rebound.

4) Blue-chip stocks are shares in large, well-known companies with a solid history of growth. They generally pay dividends.

Another way to categorize stocks is by the size of the company, as shown in its market capitalization. There are large-cap, mid-cap, and small-cap stocks. Shares in very small companies are sometimes called "microcap" stocks. The very lowest priced stocks are known as "penny stocks." These companies may have little or no earnings. Penny stocks do not pay dividends and are highly speculative.

What Are The Benefits And Risks Of Stocks?

- Stocks offer investors the greatest potential for growth (capital appreciation) over the long haul. Investors willing to stick with stocks over long periods of time, say 15 years, generally have been rewarded with strong, positive returns.

- But stock prices move down as well as up. There's no guarantee that the company whose stock you hold will grow and do well, so you can lose the money you invest in stocks.

- If a company goes bankrupt and its assets are liquidated, common stockholders are the last in line to share in the proceeds. The company's bondholders will be paid first, then holders of preferred stock. If you are a common stockholder, you get whatever is left, which may be nothing.

- Even when companies aren't in danger of failing, their stock price may fluctuate up or down. Large company stocks as a group, for example, have lost money on average about one out of every three years. If you have to sell shares on a day when the stock price is below the price you paid for the shares, you will lose money on the sale.
- Market fluctuations can be unnerving to some investors. A stock's price can be affected by factors inside the company, such as a faulty product, or by events the company has no control over, such as political or market events.
- Stocks usually are one part of an investor's holdings. If you are young and saving for a long-term goal such as retirement, you may want to hold more stocks than bonds. Investors nearing or in retirement may want to hold more bonds than stocks.
- The risks of stock holdings can be offset in part by investing in a number of different stocks. Investing in other kinds of assets that are not stocks, such as bonds, is another way to offset some of the risks of owning stocks.

How to Buy and Sell Stocks

You can buy and sell stocks through:

- A direct stock plan
- A dividend reinvestment plan
- A discount or full-service broker
- A stock fund

Direct stock plans. Some companies allow you to buy or sell their stock directly through them without using a broker. This saves on commissions, but you may have to pay other fees to the plan, including if you transfer shares to a broker to sell them. Some companies limit direct stock plans to employees of the company or existing shareholders. Some require minimum amounts for purchases or account levels.

Direct stock plans usually will not allow you to buy or sell shares at a specific market price or at a specific time. Instead, the company will buy or sell shares for the plan at set times—such as daily, weekly, or monthly—and at an average market price. Depending on the plan, you may be able to automate your purchases and have the cost deducted automatically from your savings account.

Dividend reinvestment plans. These plans allow you to buy more shares of a stock you already own by reinvesting dividend payments into the company. You must sign an agreement with the company to have this done. Check with the company or your brokerage firm to see if you will be charged for this service.

Discount or full-service broker. Brokers buy and sell shares for customers for a fee, known as a commission.

Stock funds are another way to buy stocks. These are a type of mutual fund or ETF that invests primarily in stocks. Depending on its investment objective and policies, a stock fund may concentrate on a particular type of stock, such as blue chips, large-cap value stocks, or mid-cap growth stocks. Stock funds are offered by investment companies and can be purchased directly from them or through a broker or adviser.

Understanding Fees

Buying and selling stocks entails fees. A direct stock plan or a dividend reinvestment plan may charge you a fee for that service. Brokers who buy and sell stocks for you charge a commission. A discount brokerage charges lower commissions than what you would pay at a full-service brokerage. But generally you have to research and choose investments by yourself. A full-service brokerage costs more, but the higher commissions pay for investment advice based on that firm's research.

Avoiding Fraud

Stocks in public companies are registered with the SEC and in most cases, public companies are required to file reports to the SEC quarterly and annually. Annual reports include financial statements that have been audited by an independent audit firm. Information on public companies can be found on the SEC's EDGAR system.

Bonds[52]

A bond is a debt security, similar to an IOU. Borrowers issue bonds to raise money from investors willing to lend them money for a certain amount of time. When you buy a bond, you are lending to the issuer, which may be a government, municipality, or corporation. In return, the issuer promises to pay you a specified rate of interest during the life of the bond and to repay the principal, also known as face value or par value of the bond, when it "matures," or comes due after a set period of time.

Why Do People Buy Bonds?

Investors buy bonds because:

- They provide a predictable income stream. Typically, bonds pay interest twice a year.
- If the bonds are held to maturity, bondholders get back the entire principal, so bonds are a way to preserve capital while investing.
- Bonds can help offset exposure to more volatile stock holdings.
- Companies, governments and municipalities issue bonds to get money for various things, which may include:
- Providing operating cash flow
- Financing debt
- Funding capital investments in schools, highways, hospitals, and other projects

What Types Of Bonds Are There?

- **Corporate bonds.** These are debt securities issued by private and public corporations.
- **Investment-grade.** These bonds have a higher credit rating, implying less credit risk, than high-yield corporate bonds.
- **High-yield.** These bonds have a lower credit rating, implying higher credit risk, than investment-grade bonds and, therefore, offer higher interest rates in return for the increased risk.
- **Municipal bonds**, called "munis," are debt securities issued by states, cities, counties and other government entities. Types of "munis" include:
  - o **General obligation bonds.** These bonds are not secured by any assets; instead, they are backed by the "full faith and credit" of the issuer, which has the power to tax residents to pay bondholders.

o **Revenue bonds.** Instead of taxes, these bonds are backed by revenues from a specific project or source, such as highway tolls or lease fees. Some revenue bonds are "non-recourse," meaning that if the revenue stream dries up, the bondholders do not have a claim on the underlying revenue source.

o **Conduit bonds.** Governments sometimes issue municipal bonds on behalf of private entities such as non-profit colleges or hospitals. These "conduit" borrowers typically agree to repay the issuer, who pays the interest and principal on the bonds. If the conduit borrower fails to make a payment, the issuer usually is not required to pay the bondholders.

- **U.S. Treasuries** are issued by the U.S. Department of the Treasury on behalf of the federal government. They carry the full faith and credit of the U.S. government, making them a safe and popular investment. Types of U.S. Treasury debt include:

o **Treasury Bills.** Short-term securities maturing in a few days to 52 weeks

o **Notes.** Longer-term securities maturing within ten years

o **Bonds.** Long-term securities that typically mature in 30 years and pay interest every six months

o **TIPS.** Treasury Inflation-Protected Securities are notes and bonds whose principal is adjusted based on changes in the Consumer Price Index. TIPS pay interest every six months and are issued with maturities of five, ten, and 30 years.

What Are The Benefits And Risks Of Bonds?

Bonds can provide a means of preserving capital and earning a predictable return. Bond investments provide steady streams of income from interest payments prior to maturity.

The interest from municipal bonds generally is exempt from federal income tax and also may be exempt from state and local taxes for residents in the states where the bond is issued.

As with any investment, bonds have risks. These risks include:

- **Credit risk.** The issuer may fail to timely make interest or principal payments and thus default on its bonds.
- **Interest rate risk.** Interest rate changes can affect a bond's value. If bonds are held to maturity the investor will receive the face value, plus interest. If sold before maturity, the bond may be worth more or less than the face value. Rising interest rates will make newly issued bonds more appealing to investors because the newer bonds will have a higher rate of interest than older ones. To sell an older bond with a lower interest rate, you might have to sell it at a discount.
- **Inflation risk.** Inflation is a general upward movement in prices. Inflation reduces purchasing power, which is a risk for investors receiving a fixed rate of interest.
- **Liquidity risk.** This refers to the risk that investors won't find a market for the bond, potentially preventing them from buying or selling when they want.
- **Call risk.** The possibility that a bond issuer retires a bond before its maturity date, something an issuer might do if interest rates decline, much like a homeowner might refinance a mortgage to benefit from lower interest rates.

Avoiding Fraud

Corporate bonds are securities and, if publicly offered, must be registered with the SEC. The registration of these securities can be verified using the SEC's EDGAR system. Be wary of any person who attempts to sell non-registered bonds.

Mutual Funds[53]

A mutual fund is a company that pools money from many investors and invests the money in securities such as stocks, bonds, and short-term debt. The combined holdings of the mutual fund are known as its portfolio. Investors buy shares in mutual funds. Each share represents an investor's part ownership in the fund and the income it generates.

Why Do People Buy Mutual Funds?

- Mutual funds are a popular choice among investors because they generally offer the following features:
- Professional Management. The fund managers do the research for you. They select the securities and monitor the performance.
- Diversification or "Don't put all your eggs in one basket." Mutual funds typically invest in a range of companies and industries. This helps to lower your risk if one company fails.
- Affordability. Most mutual funds set a relatively low dollar amount for initial investment and subsequent purchases.
- Liquidity. Mutual fund investors can easily redeem their shares at any time, for the current net asset value (NAV) plus any redemption fees.

What Types Of Mutual Funds Are There?

Most mutual funds fall into one of four main categories – money market funds, bond funds, stock funds, and target date funds. Each type has different features, risks, and rewards.

- Money market funds have relatively low risks. By law, they can invest only in certain high-quality, short-term investments issued by U.S. corporations, and federal, state and local governments.
- Bond funds have higher risks than money market funds because they typically aim to produce higher returns. Because there are many different types of bonds, the risks and rewards of bond funds can vary dramatically.
- Stock funds invest in corporate stocks. Not all stock funds are the same. Some examples are:

  o Growth funds focus on stocks that may not pay a regular dividend but have potential for above-average financial gains.
  o Income funds invest in stocks that pay regular dividends.
  o Index funds track a particular market index such as the Standard & Poor's 500 Index.
  o Sector funds specialize in a particular industry segment.

- Target date funds hold a mix of stocks, bonds, and other investments. Over time, the mix gradually shifts according to the fund's strategy. Target date funds, sometimes known as lifecycle funds, are designed for individuals with particular retirement dates in mind.

What Are The Benefits And Risks Of Mutual Funds?

Mutual funds offer professional investment management and potential diversification. They also offer three ways to earn money:

- **Dividend Payments.** A fund may earn income from dividends on stock or interest on bonds. The fund then pays the shareholders nearly all the income, less expenses.
- **Capital Gains Distributions.** The price of the securities in a fund may increase. When a fund sells a security that has increased in price, the fund has a capital gain. At the end of the year, the fund distributes these capital gains, minus any capital losses, to investors.
- **Increased NAV.** If the market value of a fund's portfolio increases, after deducting expenses, then the value of the fund and its shares increases. The higher NAV reflects the higher value of your investment.

All funds carry some level of risk. With mutual funds, you may lose some or all of the money you invest because the securities held by a fund can go down in value. Dividends or interest payments may also change as market conditions change.

A fund's past performance is not as important as you might think because past performance does not predict future returns. But past performance can tell you how volatile or stable a fund has been over a period of time. The more volatile the fund, the higher the investment risk.

How To Buy And Sell Mutual Funds

Investors buy mutual fund shares from the fund itself or through a broker for the fund, rather than from other investors. The price that investors pay for the mutual fund is the fund's per share net asset value plus any fees charged at the time of purchase, such as sales loads.

Mutual fund shares are "redeemable," meaning investors can sell the shares back to the fund at any time. The fund usually must send you the payment within seven days.

Before buying shares in a mutual fund, read the prospectus carefully. The prospectus contains information about the mutual fund's investment objectives, risks, performance, and expenses.

Understanding Fees

As with any business, running a mutual fund involves costs. Funds pass along these costs to investors by charging fees and expenses. Fees and expenses vary from fund to fund. A fund with high costs must perform better than a low-cost fund to generate the same returns for you.

Even small differences in fees can mean large differences in returns over time. For example, if you invested $10,000 in a fund with a 10% annual return, and annual operating expenses of 1.5%, after 20 years you would have roughly $49,725. If you invested in a fund with the same performance and expenses of 0.5%, after 20 years you would end up with $60,858.

It takes only minutes to use a mutual fund cost calculator to compute how the costs of different mutual funds add up over time and eat into your returns.

Avoiding Fraud

By law, each mutual fund is required to file a prospectus and regular shareholder reports with the SEC. Before you invest, be sure to read the prospectus and the required shareholder reports. Additionally, the investment portfolios of mutual funds are managed by separate entities known as "investment advisers" that are registered with the SEC. Always check that the investment adviser is registered before investing.

Exchange-Traded Funds (ETFs)[54]

ETFs are a type of exchange-traded investment product that must register with the SEC under the 1940 Act as either an open-end investment company (generally known as "funds") or a unit investment trust.

Like mutual funds, ETFs offer investors a way to pool their money in a fund that makes investments in stocks, bonds, or other assets and, in return, to receive an interest in that investment pool. Unlike mutual funds, however, ETF shares are traded on a national stock exchange and at market prices that may or may not be the same as the net asset value ("NAV") of the shares, that is, the value of the ETF's assets minus its liabilities divided by the number of shares outstanding.

Things To Consider Before Investing In ETFs

ETFs are not mutual funds. Generally, ETFs combine features of a mutual fund, which can be purchased or redeemed at the end of each trading day at its NAV per share, with the intraday trading feature of a closed-end fund, whose shares trade throughout the trading day at market prices.

Unlike with mutual fund shares, retail investors can only purchase and sell ETF shares in market transactions. That is, unlike mutual funds, ETFs do not sell individual shares directly to, or redeem their individual shares directly from, retail investors. Instead, ETF sponsors enter into contractual relationships with one or more financial institutions known as "Authorized Participants." Authorized Participants typically are large broker-dealers. Only Authorized Participants are permitted to purchase and redeem shares directly from the ETF, and they can do so only in large aggregations or blocks (e.g., 50,000 ETF shares) commonly called "Creation Units."

Other investors purchase and sell ETF shares in market transactions at market prices. An ETF's market price typically will be more or less than the fund's NAV per share. This is because the ETF's market price fluctuates during the trading day as a result of a variety of factors, including the underlying prices of the ETF's assets and the demand for the ETF, while the ETF's NAV is the value of the ETF's assets minus its liabilities, as calculated by the ETF at the end of each business day.

Types of ETFs

- **Index-Based ETFs**. Most ETFs trading in the marketplace are index-based ETFs. These ETFs seek to track a securities index like the S&P 500 stock index and generally invest primarily in the component securities of the index. For example, the SPDR, or "spider" ETF, which seeks to track the S&P 500 stock index, invests in most or all of the equity securities contained in the S&P 500 stock index. Some, but not all, ETFs may post their holdings on their websites on a daily basis.

- **Actively Managed ETFs.** Actively managed ETFs are not based on an index. Instead, they seek to achieve a stated investment objective by investing in a portfolio of stocks, bonds, and other assets. Unlike with an index-based ETF, an adviser of an actively managed ETF may actively buy or sell components in the portfolio on a daily basis without regard to conformity with an index.

Before investing in an ETF, you should read both its summary prospectus and its full prospectus, which provide detailed information on the ETF's investment objective, principal investment strategies, risks, costs, and historical performance (if any). The SEC's EDGAR system, as well as Internet search engines, can help you locate a specific ETF prospectus. You can also find prospectuses on the websites of the financial firms that sponsor a particular ETF, as well as through your broker.

Do not invest in something that you do not understand. If you cannot explain the investment opportunity in a few words and in an understandable way, you may need to reconsider the potential investment.

You may wish to consider seeking the advice of an investment professional. If you do, be sure to work with someone who understands your investment objectives and tolerance for risk. Your investment professional should understand complex products and be able to explain to your satisfaction whether or how they fit with your objectives.

Real Estate Investment Trusts (REITs)[55]

Real estate investment trusts ("REITs") allow individuals to invest in large-scale, income-producing real estate. A REIT is a company that owns and typically operates income-producing real estate or related assets. These may include office buildings, shopping malls, apartments, hotels, resorts, self-storage facilities, warehouses, and mortgages or loans. Unlike other real estate companies, a REIT does not develop real estate properties to resell them. Instead, a REIT buys and develops properties primarily to operate them as part of its own investment portfolio.

Why Would Somebody Invest in REITs?

REITs provide a way for individual investors to earn a share of the income produced through commercial real estate ownership – without actually having to go out and buy commercial real estate.

What Types of REITs Are There?

Many REITs are registered with the SEC and are publicly traded on a stock exchange. These are known as publicly traded REITs. Others may be registered with the SEC but are not publicly traded. These are known as non-traded REITs (also known as non-exchange traded REITs). This is one of the most important distinctions among the various kinds of REITs. Before investing in a REIT, you should understand whether or not it is publicly traded, and how this could affect the benefits and risks to you.

What Are the Benefits and Risks of REITs?

REITs offer a way to include real estate in one's investment portfolio. Additionally, some REITs may offer higher dividend yields than some other investments.

But there are some risks, especially with non-exchange traded REITs. Because they do not trade on a stock exchange, non-traded REITs involve special risks:

- **Lack of Liquidity:** Non-traded REITs are illiquid investments. They generally cannot be sold readily on the open market. If you need to sell an asset to raise money quickly, you may not be able to do so with shares of a non-traded REIT.
- **Share Value Transparency:** While the market price of a publicly traded REIT is readily accessible, it can be difficult to determine the value of a share of a non-traded REIT. Non-traded REITs typically do not provide an estimate of their value per share until 18 months after their offering closes. This may be years after you

have made your investment. As a result, for a significant time period you may be unable to assess the value of your non-traded REIT investment and its volatility.

- **Distributions May Be Paid from Offering Proceeds and Borrowings***:* Investors may be attracted to non-traded REITs by their relatively high dividend yields compared to those of publicly traded REITs. Unlike publicly traded REITs, however, non-traded REITs frequently pay distributions in excess of their funds from operations. To do so, they may use offering proceeds and borrowings. This practice, which is typically not used by publicly traded REITs, reduces the value of the shares and the cash available to the company to purchase additional assets.

- **Conflicts of Interest:** Non-traded REITs typically have an external manager instead of their own employees. This can lead to potential conflicts of interests with shareholders. For example, the REIT may pay the external manager significant fees based on the amount of property acquisitions and assets under management. These fee incentives may not necessarily align with the interests of shareholders.

How to Buy and Sell REITs

You can invest in a publicly traded REIT, which is listed on a major stock exchange, by purchasing shares through a broker. You can purchase shares of a non-traded REIT through a broker that participates in the non-traded REIT's offering. You can also purchase shares in a REIT mutual fund or REIT exchange-traded fund.

Understanding Fees and Taxes

Publicly traded REITs can be purchased through a broker. Generally, you can purchase the common stock, preferred stock, or debt security of a publicly traded REIT. Brokerage fees will apply.

Non-traded REITs are typically sold by a broker or financial adviser. Non-traded REITs generally have high up-front fees. Sales commissions and upfront offering fees usually total approximately 9 to 10 percent of the investment. These costs lower the value of the investment by a significant amount.

Special Tax Considerations

REITs pay out most of their taxable income to their shareholders. The shareholders of a REIT are responsible for paying taxes on the dividends and any capital gains they receive in connection with their investment in the REIT. Dividends paid by REITs generally are treated as ordinary income and are not entitled to the reduced tax rates on other types of corporate dividends. Consider consulting your tax adviser before investing in REITs.

Avoiding Fraud

Be wary of any person who attempts to sell REITs that are not registered with the SEC.

You can verify the registration of both publicly traded and non-traded REITs through the SEC's EDGAR system. You can also use EDGAR to review a REIT's annual and quarterly reports as well as any offering prospectus.

You should also check out the broker or investment adviser who recommends purchasing a REIT.

Commodities[56]

A commodity futures contract is an agreement to buy or sell a specific quantity of a commodity at a specified price on a particular date in the future. Metals, grains, and other food, as well as financial instruments, including U.S. and foreign currencies, are traded in the futures market. With limited exceptions, trading in futures contracts must be executed on the floor of a commodity exchange. Exchange-traded commodity futures and options provide traders with contracts of a set unit size, a fixed expiration date, and centralized clearing. In centralized clearing, a clearing corporation acts as a single counterparty to every transaction and guarantees the completion and credit worthiness of all transactions.

Anyone who trades futures with the public or gives advice about futures trading must be registered with the National Futures Association (NFA). Before investing in commodity futures, check that the individual and firm are registered.

The SEC does not regulate commodity futures. The Commodity Futures Trading Commission (CFTC) is the federal agency that regulates futures trading. The CFTC cautions investors to be wary of offers for high yield investment opportunities in futures, options, or foreign exchange, also called forex. These are common areas of fraud.

Municipal Bonds[57]

Municipal bonds (or "munis") are debt securities issued by states, cities, counties and other governmental entities to fund day-to-day obligations and to finance capital projects such as building schools, highways or sewer systems. By purchasing municipal bonds, you are in effect lending money to the bond issuer in exchange for a promise of regular interest payments, usually semi-annually, and the return of the original investment, or "principal." A municipal bond's maturity date (the date when the issuer of the bond repays the principal) may be years in the future. Short-term bonds mature in one to three years, while long-term bonds won't mature for more than a decade.

Generally, the interest on municipal bonds is exempt from federal income tax. The interest may also be exempt from state and local taxes if you reside in the state where the bond is issued. Bond investors typically seek a steady stream of income payments and, compared to stock investors, may be more risk-averse and more focused on preserving, rather than increasing, wealth. Given the tax benefits, the interest rate for municipal bonds is usually lower than on taxable fixed-income securities such as corporate bonds.

The two most common types of municipal bonds are the following:

- General obligation bonds are issued by states, cities or counties and not secured by any assets. Instead, general obligation are backed by the "full faith and credit" of the issuer, which has the power to tax residents to pay bondholders.
- Revenue bonds are not backed by government's taxing power but by revenues from a specific project or source, such as highway tolls or lease fees. Some revenue bonds are "non-recourse", meaning that if the revenue stream dries up, the bondholders do not have a claim on the underlying revenue source.

In addition, municipal borrowers sometimes issue bonds on behalf of private entities such as non-profit colleges or hospitals. These "conduit" borrowers typically agree to repay the issuer, who pays the interest and principal on the bonds. In cases where the conduit borrower fails to make a payment, the issuer usually is not required to pay the bondholders.

Where Can Investors Find Information About Municipal Bonds?

Investors wishing to research municipal bonds may access a range of information online free of charge at the Municipal Securities Rulemaking Board's Electronic Municipal Market Access (EMMA) website. Information available to you includes:

- Disclosure documents going back as early as 1990, including a bond's official statement, which is a disclosure document similar to a prospectus that includes important characteristics, such as type, yield, maturity, credit quality, call features and risk factors, as well as audited financial statements, material event notices and other continuing disclosures (including ratings changes, principal and interest payment delinquencies and non-payment related defaults).[58]
- Historical and real-time transaction price data, including information relating to a type of municipal bond called a "variable rate demand obligation" that resets its interest rate periodically. Investors should be aware that recent price information may not be available for bonds that do not trade frequently.[59]

What Are Some of the Risks of Investing in Municipal Bonds?

As with any investment, investing in municipal bonds entails risk. Investors in municipal bonds face a number of risks, specifically including:

- **Call risk.** Call risk refers to the potential for an issuer to repay a bond before its maturity date, something that an issuer may do if interest rates decline – much as a homeowner might refinance a mortgage loan to benefit from lower interest rates. Bond calls are less likely when interest rates are stable or moving higher. Many municipal bonds are "callable," so investors who want to hold a municipal bond to maturity should research the bond's call provisions before making a purchase.

- **Credit risk.** This is the risk that the bond issuer may experience financial problems that make it difficult or impossible to pay interest and principal in full (the failure to pay interest or principal is referred to as "default"). Credit ratings are available for many bonds. Credit ratings seek to estimate the relative credit risk of a bond as compared with other bonds, although a high rating does not reflect a prediction that the bond has no chance of defaulting.

- **Interest rate risk.** Bonds have a fixed face value, known as the "par" value. If bonds are held to maturity, the investor will receive the face value amount back, plus interest that may be set at a fixed or floating rate. The bond's market price will move up as interest rates move down and it will decline as interest rates rise, so that the market value of the bond may be more or less than the par value. U.S. interest rates have been low for some time. If they move higher, investors who hold a low fixed-rate municipal bond and try to sell it before it matures could lose money because of the lower market value of the bond.

- **Inflation risk.** Inflation is a general upward movement in prices. Inflation reduces purchasing power, which is a risk for investors receiving a fixed rate of interest. It also can lead to higher interest rates and, in turn, lower market value for existing bonds.

- **Liquidity risk.** This refers to the risk that investors won't find an active market for the municipal bond, potentially preventing them from buying or selling when they want and obtaining a certain price for the bond. Many investors buy municipal bonds to hold them rather than to trade them, so the market for a particular bond may not be especially liquid and quoted prices for the same bond may differ.

In Addition to the Risks, What Other Factors Should You Consider When Investing in Municipal Bonds?

- **Tax implications.** Consider consulting a tax professional to discuss the bond's tax implications, including the possibility that your bond may be subject to the federal alternative minimum tax or eligible for state income tax benefits.

- **Broker compensation.** Most brokers are compensated through a markup over the cost of the bond to the firm. This markup is usually not disclosed on your confirmation statement. If a commission is charged, it will be reported on your confirmation statement. You should ask your broker about markups and commissions.
- **The background of the broker or adviser selling the bond.** A securities salesperson must be properly licensed, and, depending on the type of business the firm conducts, his or her firm must be registered with the MSRB and with FINRA, the SEC or a state securities regulator. You can check out an investment adviser on the SEC's Investment Adviser Public Disclosure website at www.adviserinfo.sec.gov and a broker on FINRA's BrokerCheck website at www.finra.org/brokercheck. To confirm MSRB registration, you can review the MSRB's registered dealers list at http://www.msrb.org/msrb1/pqweb/registrants.asp.

Annuities[60]

An annuity is a contract between you and an insurance company that requires the insurer to make payments to you, either immediately or in the future. You buy an annuity by making either a single payment or a series of payments. Similarly, your payout may come either as one lump-sum payment or as a series of payments over time.

Why Do People Buy Annuities?

People typically buy annuities to help manage their income in retirement. Annuities provide three things:

- Periodic payments for a specific amount of time. This may be for the rest of your life, or the life of your spouse or another person.
- Death benefits. If you die before you start receiving payments, the person you name as your beneficiary receives a specific payment.
- Tax-deferred growth. You pay no taxes on the income and investment gains from your annuity until you withdraw the money.

What Kinds of Annuities Are There?

There are three basic types of annuities, fixed, variable and indexed. Here is how they work:

- **Fixed annuity.** The insurance company promises you a minimum rate of interest and a fixed amount of periodic payments. Fixed annuities are regulated by state insurance commissioners. Please check with your state insurance commission about the risks and benefits of fixed annuities and to confirm that your insurance broker is registered to sell insurance in your state.
- **Variable annuity.** The insurance company allows you to direct your annuity payments to different investment options, usually mutual funds. Your payout will vary depending on how much you put in, the rate of return on your investments, and expenses. The SEC regulates variable annuities.
- **Indexed annuity.** This annuity combines features of securities and insurance products. The insurance company credits you with a return that is based on a stock market index, such as the Standard & Poor's 500 Index. Indexed annuities are regulated by state insurance commissioners.

What Are the Benefits and Risks of Variable Annuities?

Some people look to annuities to "insure" their retirement and to receive periodic payments once they no longer receive a salary. There are two phases to annuities, the accumulation phase and the payout phase.

- During the accumulation phase, you make payments that may be split among various investment options. In addition, variable annuities often allow you to put some of your money in an account that pays a fixed rate of interest.
- During the payout phase, you get your payments back, along with any investment income and gains. You may take the payout in one lump-sum payment, or you may choose to receive a regular stream of payments, generally monthly.

All investments carry a level of risk. Make sure you consider the financial strength of the insurance company issuing the annuity. You want to be sure the company will still be around, and financially sound, during your payout phase.

Variable annuities have a number of features that you need to understand before you invest. Understand that variable annuities are designed as an investment for long-term goals, such as retirement. They are not suitable for short-term goals because you typically will pay substantial taxes and charges or other penalties if you withdraw your money early. Variable annuities also involve investment risks, just as mutual funds do.

How to Buy and Sell Annuities

Insurance companies sell annuities, as do some banks, brokerage firms, and mutual fund companies. Make sure you read and understand your annuity contract. All fees should be clearly stated in the contract. Your most important source of information about investment options within a variable annuity is the mutual fund prospectus. Request prospectuses for all the mutual fund options you might want to select. Read the prospectuses carefully before you decide how to allocate your purchase payments among the investment options.

Realize that if you are investing in a variable annuity through a tax-advantaged retirement plan, such as a 401(k) plan or an Individual Retirement Account, you will get no additional tax advantages from a variable annuity. In such cases, consider buying a variable annuity only if it makes sense because of the annuity's other features.

Note that if you sell or withdraw money from a variable annuity too soon after your purchase, the insurance company will impose a "surrender charge." This is a type of sales charge that applies in the "surrender period," typically six to eight years after you buy the annuity. Surrender charges will reduce the value of – and the return on – your investment.

Understanding Fees

You will pay several charges when you invest in a variable annuity. Be sure you understand all charges before you invest. Besides surrender charges, there are a number of other charges, including:

- **Mortality and expense risk charge.** This charge is equal to a certain percentage of your account value, typically about 1.25%

per year. This charge pays the issuer for the insurance risk it assumes under the annuity contract. The profit from this charge sometimes is used to pay a commission to the person who sold you the annuity.

- **Administrative fees.** The issuer may charge you for record keeping and other administrative expenses. This may be a flat annual fee, or a percentage of your account value.
- **Underlying fund expenses.** In addition to fees charged by the issuer, you will pay the fees and expenses for underlying mutual fund investments.
- **Fees and charges for other features.** Additional fees typically apply for special features, such as a guaranteed minimum income benefit or long-term care insurance. Initial sales loads, fees for transferring part of your account from one investment option to another, and other fees also may apply.
- **Penalties.** If you withdraw money from an annuity before you are age 59 ½, you may have to pay a 10% tax penalty to the Internal Revenue Service on top of any taxes you owe on the income.

Avoiding Fraud

Variable annuities are considered to be securities. All broker-dealers and investment advisers that sell variable annuities must be registered. Before buying an annuity from a broker or adviser, confirm that they are registered using BrokerCheck.

In most cases, the investments offered within a variable annuity are mutual funds. By law, each mutual fund is required to file a prospectus and regular shareholder reports with the SEC. Before you invest, be sure to read these materials.

Savings for Education-529 Plan[61]

A 529 plan is a tax-advantaged savings plan designed to encourage saving for future college costs. These plans, legally known as "qualified tuition plans," are sponsored by states, state agencies, or educational institutions, and are authorized by Section 529 of the Internal Revenue Code.

There are two types of 529 plans: pre-paid tuition plans and college savings plans. All 50 states and the District of Columbia sponsor at least one type of 529 plan. In addition, a group of private colleges and universities sponsor a pre-paid tuition plan.

What Are the Differences Between Pre-Paid Tuition Plans and College Savings Plans?

- Pre-paid tuition plans generally allow college savers to purchase units or credits at participating colleges and universities for future tuition and, in some cases, room and board. Most prepaid tuition plans are sponsored by state governments and have residency requirements. Many state governments guarantee investments in pre-paid tuition plans that they sponsor.
- College savings plans generally permit a college saver, also called the "account holder," to establish an account for a student (the "beneficiary") for the purpose of paying for the beneficiary's eligible college expenses.
- An account holder may typically choose among several investment options which often include stock mutual funds, bond mutual funds, and money market funds, as well as age-based portfolios that automatically shift toward a more conservative mix of investments as the beneficiary gets closer to college age.
- Withdrawals from college savings plans generally can be used at any college or university. Investments in college savings plans that invest in mutual funds are not guaranteed by state governments and are not federally insured.

The chart below shows some of the major differences between pre-paid tuition plans and college savings plans:[62]

PREPAID TUITION PLAN	COLLEGE SAVINGS PLAN
Locks in tuition prices at eligible public and private colleges and universities.	No lock on college costs.
All plans cover tuition and mandatory fees only. Some plans allow you to purchase a room & board option or use excess tuition credits for other qualified expenses.	Covers all "qualified higher education expenses," including: tuition, room & board, mandatory fees, books, and computers (if required).
Most plans set lump sum and installment payments prior to purchase based on age of beneficiary and number of years of college tuition purchased.	No state guarantee. Most investment options are subject to market risk. Your investment may make no profit or even decline in value.
Most plans have age/grade limit for beneficiary.	No age limits. Open to adults and children.
Most state plans require either owner or beneficiary of plan to be a state resident.	No residency requirement. However, nonresidents may only be able to purchase some plans through financial advisers or brokers.
Most plans have limited enrollment period.	Enrollment opens all year.

How Does Investing in a 529 Plan Affect Federal and State Income Taxes?

- Investing in a 529 plan may offer college savers special tax benefits. Earnings in 529 plans are not subject to federal tax, and in most cases, state tax, provided you use withdrawals for eligible college expenses, such as tuition and room and board.
- However, if you withdraw money from a 529 plan and do not use it for an eligible college expense, you generally will be subject to income tax and a 10% federal tax penalty on earnings. Many states offer state income tax or other benefits, such as matching grants, for investing in a 529 plan. But you may only be eligible for these benefits if you participate in a 529 plan sponsored by your state of residence. Just a few states allow residents to deduct contributions to any 529 plan from state income tax returns.

Does Investing in a 529 Plan Impact Financial Aid Eligibility?

Investing in a 529 plan generally will reduce a student's eligibility to participate in need-based financial aid. Assets held in pre-paid tuition plans and college savings plans have been treated similarly for federal financial aid purposes since mid-2006. Both are treated as parental assets when calculating the expected family contribution toward college costs.

What Fees and Expenses Will I Pay If I Invest in a 529 Plan?

• It is important to understand the fees and expenses associated with 529 plans because they lower your returns. Fees and expenses will vary based on the type of plan. Prepaid tuition plans typically charge enrollment and administrative fees. In addition to "loads" for broker-sold plans, college savings plans may charge enrollment fees, annual maintenance fees, and asset management fees.

• Some of these fees are collected by the state sponsor of the plan, and some are collected by the financial services firms hired by the state sponsor to manage the 529 program. Some college savings plans will waive or reduce some of these fees if you maintain a large account balance, participate in an automatic contribution plan, or are a resident of the state sponsoring the 529 plan.

Is There Any Way to Purchase a 529 Plan But Avoid Some of the Extra Fees?

Direct-Sold College Savings Plans. States offer college savings plans that residents and, in many cases, non-residents can invest in without paying a "load," or sales fee. This type of plan, which you can buy directly from the plan's sponsor or program manager without the assistance of a broker, is generally less expensive because it waives or does not charge sales fees that may apply to broker-sold plans. For information, contact the plan's sponsor or program manager or visit the plan's website. Websites such as the one maintained by the College Savings Plan Network, as well as a number of commercial websites, provide links to most 529 plan websites.

What Questions Should I Ask Before I Invest in a 529 Plan?

- Is the plan available directly from the state or plan sponsor?
- Does the plan offer special benefits for state residents?
- Would I be better off investing in my state's plan or another plan?
- Does my state's plan offer tax advantages or other benefits for investment in the plan it sponsors?
- If my state's plan charges higher fees than another state's plan, do the tax advantages or other benefits offered by my state outweigh the benefit of investing in another state's less expensive plan?
- What fees are charged by the plan?
- How much of my investment goes to compensating a broker?
- Under what circumstances does the plan waive or reduce certain fees?
- What are the plan's withdrawal restrictions?
- Which colleges and universities participate in the plan?
- What types of college expenses are covered by the plan?
- What types of investment options are offered by the plan?
- How long are contributions held before being invested?
- What limitations apply to the plan?
- When can an account holder change investment options, switch beneficiaries, or transfer ownership of the account to another account holder?
- Who is the program manager? How has the plan performed in the past?

Tax Implications for Investments

Tax implications for investments can vary from one investment to another. With so many investment options and changing tax laws, it is best to work with a tax professional. To help you, consider discussing your tax planning with professionals who are Certified Public Accountants (CPA) or Enrolled Agents (EA). Investopedia.com defines these two as:

(CPA):[63] Certified Public Accountant (CPA) is a designation given by the American Institute of Certified Public Accountants to those who pass an exam and meet work experience requirements. For the most part, the accounting industry is self-regulated. The CPA designation ensures that professional standards for the industry are enforced.

(EA):[64] An enrolled agent (EA) is a tax professional allowed to represent taxpayers in matters concerning the Internal Revenue Service (IRS). EAs must pass an examination or have sufficient experience as an IRS employee and pass a background check. Enrolled agents first appeared in 1884 because of issues arising with Civil War loss claims.

Chapter 7 will go into more details of taxation. Here, I want you to be aware of the tax treatment for capital gains. In general, when you sell an asset, the profit or loss is considered a capital gain or loss. The tax rate will depend on whether or not you sold the asset before or after one year of owning it. If it is less than one year, the capital gain is considered to be "short term" so the tax rate will be the same as your ordinary income. If it is after one year, it is considered "long-term" capital gains so that it will be taxed at a fixed 15% rate for most people. There are exceptions and possible future changes, so this is why it is important to work with your trusted tax professional I just mentioned. However, I wanted you to be aware of this so you have a foundation and can start planning for taxes on your investments.

My Best Investment Recommendation

Seek a Mentor & Be an Apprentice. The best way to learn any important skill such as investing is to become an apprentice and work with a mentor. If you want to invest in real estate, seek out a trustworthy and successful real estate investor. If you want to build businesses, seek out a trustworthy and successful entrepreneur. If you want to invest in the markets, seek out a trustworthy and successful market investor. This is how you truly learn. The best do this. The best did this. The best is Warren Buffet, and he started as a student and become an apprentice.[65]

Warren Buffett is considered by many to be the greatest investor of all time, and he is currently the second richest person in the world. But he couldn't have achieved such success if he didn't have the right person to learn from when he was starting out. In 1949, at age 19, Warren Buffett found Benjamin Graham's book, *The Intelligent Investor*, and it changed his life. He learned that Ben Graham taught at Columbia University, so within a year or so, Warren applied and was accepted to Columbia.

By his second semester at school, he was able to personally learn from and get to know Ben, his professor. He was the only person to have received an A+ in Ben's class. Upon graduation from Columbia, Warren wanted to work for Ben but both Ben and Warren's father advised him not to work on Wall Street after graduation. Warren offered to work for Ben for free but it was turned down. Determined, Warren came home to Omaha where he worked with his father and began investing on his own. However, his investments were not successful. During this time, Warren married Susie and had a daughter. To save money, they used a dresser drawer as their daughter's crib. About two years later, Ben Graham called Warren, who immediately flew to New York to meet with Ben. This time, Warren got what he wanted, and he began working for Ben. That's how Warren Buffett began to master his investing skills and became the great investor of all time, by being an apprentice to Benjamin Graham.

Chapter Seven

BORROWING MONEY

"There's nothing inappropriate about having debt in America. I mean, Berkshire has debt, and it's helped us grow over time. And it's when debt gets out of control that you worry."-*Warren Buffett*

Income Statement		Balance Sheet	
Income	Expense	Assets	**Liability**
1. Income A	1. Expense A	1. Asset A	1. Debt 1
2. Income B	2. Expense 2	2. Asset B	2. Debt 2
3. Income C	3. Expense 3	3. Asset C	3. Debt 3
Total Income: $ABC	Total Expense: $123	Total Asset: $ABC	Total Liability: **$123**
Company: Net Profit/Net Loss (Total Income-Total Expense) Net Profit: $		Company: Owner's Equity (Total Asset-Total Liability) Owner's Equity: $	
Individual: Net Savings/Net Burn (Total Income-Total Expense) Net Savings: $		Individual: Net Worth (Total Asset-Total Liability) Net Worth: $	

THIS CHAPTER IS ALL ABOUT Liabilities, specifically financial liabilities. This is the final piece that completes the four sections of income, expense, assets, and liabilities. Within financial liabilities, the biggest are mortgage loans, student loans, auto loans, business loans, and credit accounts like credit cards. Unpaid tax is also a liability. The term that is commonly used to describe these types of financial liabilities is "debt." It is not a word many people who are struggling with it like. However, those that leverage debt in a smart way continue to borrow more. As you are aware, the difference between good and bad debt is: bad debt has you work for it while good debt works for you. In this chapter, you will learn how to borrow money, reduce debt, and do your taxes.

Borrowing Money

To effectively borrow money, you need to understand your credit history and score, types of loans, and how to avoid predatory lending.

Credit History And Score

Just imagine you are a bank and a person named Bob asks you to lend him some money. He is 19 years old. Before you agree to lend Bob money, would you be interested in knowing whether he had borrowed money from other people before you? If he had, how much did other people lend him? Has he been paying them? Have his payments been on time? Certainly, you would want this information. This is the essence of a person's credit history, and based on that history, a credit score is calculated and reviewed to make it easier to qualify a borrower before making a lending decision. This is why it is important to understand how to start building credit, avoid activities that hurt your credit score, and repair your credit when it is damaged. I'll review each to help you.

Building Credit History

When you are starting out, you have no history, so it is difficult to secure the first line of credit without any data to help convince the lender of your creditworthiness. Two effective options are to open a secured credit account and to get a co-signer.

- **Opening a Secured Credit Account.** This is often done through a bank or credit union. With a secured account, you give money to the bank to hold as security for a credit account for you. This way, the bank will no longer see you as a risky borrower. Returning to our friend Bob, you as the bank run a credit report on Bob and learn that he has no credit history. You suggest a secured credit card account and ask Bob to deposit $300 into an account. After Bob makes his deposit, you then give him a secured credit card with a credit limit of $300. After about six months of Bob using his secured credit card, you will review whether Bob has used his card responsibly. If he has, you can offer Bob an unsecured credit card, and Bob can close his secured credit account and get his $300 deposit back.

- **Using a Co-Signer.** If you have no credit history, the bank may ask a person with well-established credit history to co-sign the account with you. Meaning, you leverage another person's credit to build your own. The risk for the bank is now reduced because the bank makes a decision based on a person who has a history. The bigger risk is taken by the person co-signing. If the new borrower does not use the credit card responsibly, the co-signer is personally affected because he is legally responsible for the account.

Building & Maintaining Credit

Once you have successfully opened your credit account, whether secured or unsecured, it is critical to build and maintain your credit in a responsible way. Banks can quickly gauge how responsible you are with using credit by looking at your credit score. Your credit score is a number that analyzes your credit history. This score makes it easy for lenders to review your creditworthiness without having to review your years of credit history line by line. Certainly, they can do that if they wish, but the credit score is a quick way to analyze the borrower. The higher the number, the better the credit history a person has. Another name for credit score is FICO® scores which was developed by Fair, Isaac and Company, Inc. (FICO). It is the most commonly used scoring system; FICO scores range from 300 to 850. Most people score in the 600s and 700s.[66] As you build and maintain your credit history in a way that increases your credit score, it helps to know the five factors that go into determining the score.

1) **Payment History.** Pay your bills on time. Late payments hurt your score. If you file for bankruptcy, it hurts your score for many years. The same is true of a home foreclosure. (Remember that foreclosure happens when the bank repossesses a house if the borrower doesn't pay the mortgage).

2) **Balances Outstanding.** Remember Bob, who got a $300 credit line from you, the bank? Let's assume he uses all $300 of it to pay for groceries and gas. When the bill comes, he sees a minimum payment due of $25 and a balance of $300. As you already know, it is not wise to pay the minimum. Bob is smart, and he elects to pay the balance in full. Thus, his outstanding

balance is zero. The higher the balance you do not pay off, the more it can lower your credit score. For example, let's pretend Bob accidentally elected to pay the minimum instead. He is now officially carrying debt! Bob's debt is close to $300 on a $300 credit line. The term for this is "Debt-to-Credit" ratio. The higher the debt to the credit limit ratio, the worse it looks for the borrower to lenders.

3) **Length of Your Credit History.** Like building any reputation, building a credit history takes time. The longer and more consistent you are with borrowing and paying debt off, the better. This is why banks usually wait six months to reevaluate creditworthiness like you did with Bob.

4) **Applications for New Credit Accounts.** Applying to borrow money at too many places and opening too many new accounts in a short period of time can reflect negatively on your score.

5) **Types of Credit Accounts (mortgages, car loans, credit cards).** The type of accounts you have open also factors into your score. It demonstrates your ability to handle different types of credit. The key is how you are paying each of them. The more you pay off, the more favorable your score will be.

It's a recommended practice to review your credit report often, but at least once a year. Know your own credit history and score before lenders pull your credit so that you are prepared to answer any questions your lender may ask you. You can do so for free. According to the Federal Trade Commission, you are entitled to one free copy of your credit report every 12 months from each of the three nationwide credit reporting companies. Order online from annualcreditreport.com, the only authorized website for free credit reports, or call 1-877-322-8228.

Repairing Damaged Credit

For various reasons including identity theft, you may need to repair your credit. You can find government-approved organizations that can help you at www.usdoj.gov/ust, the website of the U.S. Trustee Program. Be wary of credit counseling organizations that claim to be government-approved but don't appear on the list of approved organizations.

Reputable credit counseling organizations can help you develop a budget, manage your money and debts, and provide free educational materials and training. The counselors there are trained and certified in the areas of budgeting, money and debt management, and consumer credit.

WHO Score

When you are just starting out as a student, you will have little to no ability to borrow money. If you can, it will be limited to a smaller amount. However, this should never limit you from leveraging money for "good debt" reasons. This is where your WHO Score can be more valuable than your Credit Score

Let me share a personal story with you. I had just graduated from high school, and I wanted to invest in a real estate property that I could buy and quickly sell for immediate capital gains. I had no money, and my family didn't have money either, so I didn't bother asking them. Instead, I asked my high school Key Club regional advisor and Kiwanian to lend me the money I needed to make the real estate investment. When I asked him to lend me $40,000, he asked me when I needed it. I replied, "immediately, and I will give you a 12% return on your money within ninety days." He paused and simply said, "because I know WHO you are, I am going to trust you." I was Key Club president, a group with over 200 members, and I volunteered 10+ hours a week. It did not go unnoticed by him. He wrote me the check. That day, I learned that my WHO score would be more valuable than any other score. In ninety days, I paid him back the $40,000 plus $5,000 (the 12% return on his investment in me). I netted $15,000 on that deal.

Many experienced lenders know that people are more than just numbers on a sheet of paper. Your WHO score is about your personal credibility, and it shows more than any credit score can.

In networking, it is often said, "it is not what you know, but who you know." I would like further build upon that from my experience. It is not what you know or who you know. It is who knows you, and what they know about you, that matters.

Types of Loans

Loans come in many forms, but the key loans you will most likely work with are student loans, mortgages, auto loans, credit cards, and business loans. I will cover each one for you.

Student Loans

Student loans are the fastest growing type of debt. They have surpassed credit card debt and auto debt to become the second largest debt behind mortgages.[67] Unlike scholarships and grants, student loans must be paid back. Even in bankruptcy, student loans are not washed away. Thus, it is more important than ever to understand this type of debt, so you are not blindsided by it. You have two choices for student loans: federal or private.

Federal loans. This type of loan is administered by the federal government on a financial need basis. Meaning, the qualification is simply "need," not "ability to repay." The government makes these loans available because it believes in investing in its people with higher education. The higher the education of its citizens, the greater the human capital it has to make the overall country better and produce more value.

It is important to get the most up to date information, so please visit studentaid.ed.gov to know what kind of aid you qualify for and to be aware of any new federal programs that might help you.

Private loans: These are offered by private banks and financial institutions. Your interest rate and eligibility will be based on your credit score, but you can apply with a parent or guardian as a co-signer. These loans often come with less generous repayment options and higher interest rates than federal loans.

The key difference between federal and private student loans is that federal student loans are made or guaranteed by the Department of Education.

Federal student loans can be better in these ways, according to the Consumer Financial Protection Bureau:[68]

- In some cases, the federal government will subsidize-pay the interest on-your federal student loan while you are in school.
- Your interest rate for a federal student loan is generally fixed, not variable; most private student loans carry variable interest rates.
- Federal student loans allow you to limit the amount you must repay each month based on your income.
- For borrowers pursuing careers in public service, loan forgiveness on federal student loans may be available after ten years.

Federal student loans also feature other important borrower protections, including:

- Options to delay or temporarily forgo payments (like deferment and forbearance)
- Discharge upon a borrower's death
- Discharge upon permanent disability (with certain limitations)

But the consequences of defaulting on a federal student loan are serious:

- Your wages may be garnished without a court order; and
- You can lose out on your tax refund or Social Security check (funds would be applied toward your defaulted student loan).

Private student loans are any student loans that are not federal student loans. These loans do not offer the flexible repayment terms or borrower protections of federal student loans. Private student loans are not funded or subsidized by the federal government; instead, they are funded by banks, credit unions, or other types of lenders.

The bank or lender – not the federal government – sets interest rates, loan limits, terms, and conditions of private student loans. Your ability to qualify for and borrow via a private student loan may be based on numerous factors that can include your credit history, whether or not you choose to have a co-signer, your co-signer's credit history, your choice of school, and your course of study.

While private student loan structures vary, they generally differ from federal student loans in several ways that may include:

- Variable interest rates that can rise during the life of the loan— which can substantially increase your payment
- Fewer options to reduce or postpone payments
- Less flexible repayment options

Mortgage Loans

Mortgage loans are used to buy real estates such as houses and buildings. Mortgages are the often the largest debt a person holds, but their size doesn't make them bad. This type of debt can be extremely good and very profitable (as you should already know from earlier chapters) because real estate is an asset that can produce both income and capital gains.

Why would institutions let you borrow so much? This is an important question to ask because it is a large amount of money that is given to you to use. The reason why banks and many institutions let you borrow so much is that the loan is secured by the real estate property itself. This collateral makes mortgage loans secured debt. If the borrower doesn't pay the loan, the lender takes back the real estate and sells it to recover their investment. As you know, this is called a foreclosure. This is how the lender balances its risk. Additionally, the lender also factors in the risk that the real estate value may decrease after it loans you the money. The lender understands that it may not sell the house at a price high enough to cover the amount loaned to you. Thus, to further protect their investment, they require the borrower to make a down payment. A down payment is basically putting "skin in the game," where the borrower also needs to invest cash rather than getting all of the money from a lender. The more the borrower can put "down" in cash toward the house, the less the lender needs to lend and lower the overall risk of lending. Usually, the lender wants the borrower to put 20% down so that if the lender needs to sell the house in the future, it will have a better chance of getting the full amount of money back. Even if the house goes down in value by 20%, the lender is still able to cover their investment. The bank can still lose money on the deal if the house goes down more than 20%, but it could also make more money if the house has appreciated. It is the risk management of the lender to require a 20% buffer as a standard. A lender may require a larger down payment for a riskier borrower. If you don't have 20% to put down to buy a property, you can put less, but it will increase your risk and your interest rate.

Key Information and Strategies To Help Securing A Mortgage

- **Credit score plays a big role in mortgages.** Unless the borrower can pay cash in full, lenders are usually involved, and they base their decisions on credit scores to determine your creditworthiness. The higher your score, the lower risk you will be for the lender, and it will help lower your down payment amount as well as your monthly payment.
- **Interest Rate.** The interest rate is heavily dependent on your credit score and down payment amount as well as the overall economy. This rate essentially can make or break a real estate

deal for the borrower because the higher the rate, the higher the monthly mortgage payment. If the borrower is investing in this property to rent, the mortgage payment must be lower than the rental income to produce positive monthly income. Qualifying for a lower interest rate means a lower monthly mortgage payment and higher monthly rental income.

- **Fixed versus Variable Term.** In addition to the length of years the borrower selects, the borrower may choose to have fixed interest rate or variable interest rate on the mortgage. Fixed interest locks the interest rate for the full duration of the term – either 10 years, 15 years, or 30 years. Variable rates adjust with the market and can go up or down, making the monthly mortgage payment a variable payment. Certainly, the risk associated with a variable rate mortgage is that the rate can increase so much that is causes the borrower not to be able to pay and the lender can foreclose on the house. Fixed rates stay the same regardless of the market rate going up or down. However, if the rate does go down, the borrower may choose to refinance and get a new, lower rate. To refinance is to basically redo the mortgage as if the borrower is buying the house again in order to change the term length and/ or rate.

- **Proof of income is required to qualify for a mortgage.** Lenders want to ensure that you have the income to pay your mortgage loan over the long term. To judge that your income is stable, lenders usually want two years of income tax returns to show your earning power and income stability, but that is not always required. For example, fresh college graduates may have just started working and earning monthly income that can support a mortgage. As long as the borrower can show employment strength and convince the lender that his/her employment is stable with income to pay the loan for the long term, it may work. Lenders may look at your academic degree and check if your employment is related to your academic degree. If it is, it certainly indicates more employment strength and stability. Furthermore, you can ask your employer to write a letter to your lender to show that your employer sees you as a great asset and that your employment with them is going to be long term.

- **Repayment ability is calculated based on your debt-to-income ratio.** This directly shows the lender whether or not the borrower has the ability to pay the mortgage payment. If the borrower is buying the real estate as an "owner-occupied" asset, then the debt-to-income ratio is calculated using the borrower's income. If the borrower is buying the real estate as an "investment" to be rented out, then the rental income will be also considered in the debt-to-income ratio. Generally, lenders want the total debt–to-income ratio to be no more than 40% of income. The lender adds up all of your monthly debt payments, including the new mortgage payment, to see if that total is at or less than 40% of your income. If the new mortgage payment caused the borrower's debt-to-income ratio to rise above 40%, the lender would require the borrower to reduce the debt-to-income ratio by paying off current outstanding debt, making a higher down payment to reduce the loan amount, or buying the property at a lower price; otherwise, the borrower would be disqualified.

- **Monthly mortgage payments are based on interest rate, loan size, and the length of the loan term.** The terms are generally ten years, 15 years, or 30 years. The longer the term, the lower the monthly payment for the same sized loan because the loan is stretched over a longer period of time. The shorter the term, the higher the payment as the payback time is condensed. The main benefit of a shorter term is paying less interest. However, best practice is to ensure there is no repayment penalty so the borrower may pay off the loan off sooner to pay less total interest. To help you estimate your mortgage payment, consider using a mortgage calculator. It makes it quick and easy for you. Once you have your mortgage payment calculated, including property taxes and maintenance fees, you can compare it to your rental cost to see if it makes more sense to buy a house or continue renting. Just remember that rental money is gone once you pay it. Mortgage payments go to pay down the mortgage and build equity in the home, so not all of it is gone. Plus, the house may increase in value so you can sell it for capital gains. Renting doesn't give you that control and opportunity.

- **Special Qualifying Conditions. Homeownership is the American dream for many.** The government does have programs to assist people, such as offering mortgage programs with lower down payments. Instead of 20% down, the borrower may put as little as 3.5% down. To learn more about lower down payment mortgages, please visit Hud.gov for information on Federal Housing Administration (FHA) loans. However, since the down payment is lower, the risk is also higher for the lender. As a tradeoff, the lender will require the borrower who puts less than 20% down to buy "private mortgage insurance." Private Mortgage Insurance (PMI) is a specialty insurance policy, provided by private insurers, to protect lenders against potential loss if a borrower defaults. PMI is paid monthly, usually for about five years (sixty monthly payments) and is a percentage of the loan amount. The bigger the mortgage loan, the more PMI the borrower will pay.

Auto Loans

Behind mortgage and student loans in total consumer debt are auto debts.[69] As you already know from Chapter 5, auto loans are the gateway debt, as cars are often a student's first big purchase. Choosing how much to spend, which car to buy, and how much car debt to take on will set you on a certain financial path, so understanding how car debt works will help you make the best decision for yourself, whether that is to completely avoid it or to be smart about using it.

If you have decided on a car that you don't have the money to buy and need financing, you have two options: borrow from the dealer (dealer financing) or a bank (direct financing).

Dealer Financing

This is often the default choice and perceived to be the "only" choice for car buyers. The reason is that the financing is offered by the car dealership and it is very convenient for the buyer. However, as with most conveniences, it comes with a price or trades off. In some cases with dealer financing, it isn't really the dealers themselves who lend you the money. The car dealer acts as the middleman between you and the actual lender. The dealer makes money off the spread – i.e. they'll quote you a 5% interest rate, but the actual lender charges 4%-the dealer earns the 1% difference. Before you agree to provide your Social Security number and other sensitive financial information to the dealer, do your research and find out all of your lending options, and then choose the option that is most reputable who gives you the best rate. If you are being pressured and rushed, that's a clear signal to stop and consider whether you are being forced into a deal that's not favorable to you. Give yourself at least 24 hours to do more research, and always remember that you can come back. When I am in a high-pressure situation, I remind myself that: "Higher Emotions = Lower Intelligence." Then, I give myself time to let my logic kick in.

Direct Financing

This is best done BEFORE going into a car dealership. Meaning, you first visit the banks, credit unions, or any other financial institutions to shop around for the best lending offer. Avoid having each prospective lender run your credit by not giving them your Social Security number. Each time your credit is run, your credit score will go down by a few points. Inquiries lower your score because they suggest you are trying to borrow money from many different people. It makes you appear riskier. My personal limit is two times when doing my research and shopping around and then maybe a time for my chosen option. When working directly with the lender rather than using the car dealership, you may have more options with better interest rates. You will know exactly how much you will pay per month and how much you are qualified to borrow. This number gives you your "limit" for the total price of the car and helps you select which car is financially best for you. Certainly, you don't need to, nor should you, borrow the maximum amount you are offered. Doing so will only increase your debt and start you off on a bad path financially. Knowing this will save you time and prevent you from having to work with car dealerships that push you into a more expensive car and more expensive financing to make more money. Furthermore, as an added benefit to going directly to lenders, they may have much lower prices on extended warranties or protection plans. By making this your first step in buying a car, you can save a lot of money and headaches.

Auto Loan Monthly Payment Calculation

Similar to mortgage loans, besides the actual loan amount, your monthly auto loan payment depends on the interest rate, down payment amount, credit score, and how many years (term) you want to pay. Just like for mortgages, use an auto loan calculator to determine your estimated monthly auto loan payment and how much interest you will pay in total on the loan. Similar to choosing between renting or buying a house, you can now compare the total cost of leasing a car versus the total cost to buy a car. Just remember, with the auto loan, you will have the car at the end of the term.

Credit Cards

As the fourth largest consumer debt, credit cards often target graduating high school students who recently turned eighteen and follow them throughout their college years.[70] One of the key reasons credit card companies target students is because students are the biggest opportunity for new customers to drive growth. Companies are eager to let you borrow money, but credit cards can be dangerous for those who are financially ignorant and undisciplined. By understanding how credit cards can work for you, they can become a great tool for you.

Visa, MasterCard, Discover, and American Express are the four major credit card companies. And among them, they offer a few different types of credit cards:

- **Store Credit Cards.** Stores want more loyalty from their customers, so they offer an "easy to get" credit card to use at their store only. The store also gives special discounts and offers to encourage more spending with their store credit cards
- **Secured Credit Cards.** As we discussed earlier, this is for anyone who has no credit and wants to build a history. However, this can also be used by borrowers to rebuild a damaged credit score.
- **Charge Cards.** These cards require you to pay the balance off in full when you receive each monthly statement.

Credit cards make money in many different ways, but the primary ways are through interest charges, annual fees, and late fees. Since these credit loans are easier to get approved for than other loans, interest rates are naturally higher to compensate for the higher risk. Usual rates are closer to 20% annually and can be upwards of 30%. Credit cards often allow borrowers to get cash advances, but they charge a fee plus high interest for that privilege – usually a different interest rate than the regular balance. The only way credit cards DON'T make money from their borrower is for the borrower to pay off the balance between the time he receives the monthly statement and when the grace period ends. The grace period is often two to three weeks after receiving the statement and describes the period during which a borrower can pay the money owed before it accrues interest and financing charges. The due date is printed on the statement. Again, make sure not to pay the minimum amount due, as I discussed in Chapter 3. In my opinion, "Minimum Payments" should be a bad word.

Business Loans

A great resource for getting a business loan is the Small Business Administration (SBA). Their website is SBA.gov. The SBA was created in 1953 as an independent agency of the federal government to aid, counsel, assist and protect the interests of small business concerns, to preserve free competitive enterprise, and to maintain and strengthen the overall economy of our nation. Below is information directly from SBA.gov.

Borrowing Money for Your Business [With the SBA]71

After you have developed a cash flow analysis and determined when your business will make profit, you may decide you need additional funding. Borrowing money is one of the most common sources of funding for a small business, but obtaining a loan isn't always easy. Before you approach a lender for a loan, you will need to understand the factors the bank will use to evaluate your application.

There are two types of financing: equity financing and debt financing. When looking for money, you must consider your company's debt-to-equity ratio. This ratio is the relation between dollars you have borrowed and dollars you have invested in your business. The more money owners have invested in their business, the easier it is to obtain financing.

If your firm has a high ratio of equity to debt, you should probably seek debt financing. However, if your company has a high proportion of debt to equity, experts advise that you should increase your ownership capital (equity investment) for additional funds. This will prevent you from being over-leveraged to the point of jeopardizing your company's survival.

Equity Financing

Equity financing (or equity capital) is money raised by a company in exchange for a share of ownership in the business. Ownership accounts for owning shares of stock outright or having the right to convert other financial instruments into stock. Equity financing allows a business to obtain funds without incurring debt, or without having to repay a specific amount of money at a particular time.

Most small or growth-stage businesses use limited equity financing. Equity often comes from investors such as friends, relatives, employees, customers, or industry colleagues. The most common source of equity funding comes from venture capitalists. These are institutional risk takers and may be groups of wealthy individuals, government-assisted sources, or major financial institutions. Most specialize in one or a few closely related industries.

Debt Financing

Debt financing means borrowing money that must be repaid over a period of time, usually with interest. Debt financing can be either short-term, with full repayment due in less than one year, or long-term, with repayment due over a period greater than one year. The lender does not gain an ownership interest in the business, and debt obligations are typically limited to repaying the loan with interest. Loans are often secured by some or all of the assets of the company. In addition, lenders commonly require the borrower's personal guarantee in case of default. This ensures that the borrower has a sufficient personal interest at stake in the business.

Loans can be obtained from many different sources, including banks, savings and loans, credit unions, commercial finance companies, and SBA-guaranteed loans. State and local governments have many programs that encourage the growth of small businesses. Family members, friends, and former associates are all potential sources, especially when capital requirements are smaller.

Traditionally, banks have been the major source of small business funding. The principal role of banks includes short-term loans, seasonal lines of credit, and single-purpose loans for machinery and equipment.

Banks generally have been reluctant to offer long-term loans to small firms. SBA's guaranteed lending programs encourage banks and non-bank lenders to make long-term loans to small firms by reducing their risk and leveraging the funds they have available.

Ability to Repay

The ability (or capacity) to repay the funds you receive from a lender must be justified in your loan package. Banks want to see two sources of repayment—cash flow from the business as well as a secondary source such as collateral. The lender reviews the past financial statements of a business to analyze its cash flow.

Generally, banks are more comfortable offering assistance to businesses that have been in existence for a number of years and have a proven financial track record. If the business has consistently made a profit and that profit can cover the payment of additional debt, it is likely that the loan will be approved. If however, the business is a start-up or has been operating marginally and has an opportunity to grow, it is necessary to prepare a thorough loan package with a detailed explanation including how the business will be able to repay the loan.

Credit History

When a small business requests a loan, one of the first things a lender looks at is personal and business credit history. So before you even start the process of preparing a loan request, you want to make sure you have good credit.

Get your personal credit report from one of the credit bureaus, such as TransUnion, Equifax or Experian. You should initiate this step well in advance of seeking a loan. Personal credit reports may contain errors or be out of date, and it can take three to four weeks for errors to be corrected. It is up to you to see that corrections are made, so make sure you check regularly on progress. You want to make sure that when a lender pulls your credit report, all the errors have been corrected and your history is up to date.

Once you obtain your credit report, check to make sure that all personal information, including your name, Social Security number and address is correct. Then carefully examine the rest of the report, which contains a list of all the credit you obtained in the past such as credit cards, mortgages, student loans and information on how you paid that credit. Any item indicating that you have had a problem in paying will be toward the top of the list. These are the credits that may affect your ability to obtain a loan.

If you have been late by a month on an occasional payment, this probably will not adversely affect your credit. But it is likely that you will have difficulty in obtaining a loan if you are continuously late in paying your credit, have a credit that was never paid, have a judgment against you, or have declared bankruptcy in the last seven years.

A person may have a period of bad credit as a result of divorce, medical crisis, or some other significant event. If you can show that your credit was good before and after this event and that you have tried to pay back those debts, you should be able to obtain a loan. It is best if you write an explanation of your credit problems and how you have rectified them, and attach this to your credit report in your loan package.

Each credit bureau has a slightly different way of presenting your credit information. Contact the bureau you used for more specific information how to read your credit report. If you need additional help in interpreting or evaluating your credit report, ask your accountant or a local banker.

Equity Investment

Don't be misled into thinking that a start-up business can obtain all financing through conventional or special loan programs. Financial institutions want to see a certain amount of equity in a business.

Equity can be built up through retained earnings or by the injection of cash from either the owner or investors. Most banks want to see that the total liabilities or debt of a business is not more than four times the amount of equity. So if you want a loan for your business, make sure that there is enough equity in the company to leverage that loan.

Owners usually must put some of their own money into the business to get a loan. The amount of financing depends on the type of loan, purpose and terms. Most banks want the owner to put in at least 20 to 40 percent of the total request.

Having the right debt to equity ratio does not guarantee your business will get a loan. There are a number of other factors used to evaluate a business, such as net worth, which is the amount of equity in a business, which is often a combination of retained earnings and owner's equity.

Collateral

When a financial institution gives a loan, it wants to make sure it will get its money back. That is why a lender usually requires a second source of repayment called collateral. Collateral is personal and business assets that can be sold in case the cash generated by the small business is not sufficient to repay the loan. Every loan program requires at least some collateral. If a potential borrower has no collateral, he/she will need a co-signer who has collateral to pledge. Otherwise, it may be difficult to obtain a loan.

The value of collateral is not based on market value; rather, it is discounted to take into account the value that would be lost if the assets had to be liquidated. This table gives a general approximation of how different forms of collateral are valued by a typical lender and the SBA:

COLLATERAL TYPE	LENDER	SBA
House	Market Value x 0.75 -Mortgage balance	Market Value x 0.80 -Mortgage balance
Car	Not applicable	Not applicable
Truck & Heavy Equipment	Depreciated Value x 0.50	Same
Office Equipment	Not applicable	Not applicable
Furniture & Fixtures	Depreciated Value x 0.50	Same
Inventory: Perishables	Not applicable	Not applicable
Jewelry	Not applicable	Not applicable
Other	10%-50%	10%-50%
Receivables	Under 90 days x 0.75	Under 90 days x 0.50
Stocks & Bonds	50%-90%	50%-90%
Mutual Funds	Not applicable	Not applicable
Individual Retirement Account (IRA)	Not applicable	Not applicable
Certificate of Deposit (CD)	100%	100%

Collateral Coverage Ratio

The bank will calculate your collateral coverage ratio as part of the loan evaluation process. This ratio is calculated by dividing the total discounted collateral value by the total loan request.

Management Experience

Managerial expertise is a critical element in the success of any business. In fact, poor management is most frequently cited as the reason businesses fail. Lenders will be looking closely at your education and experience as well as that of your key managers.

To strengthen your management skills, SBA offers a wide range of free, online training courses. You can also get management advice from counselors at your local SCORE office. [SCORE is a nonprofit association dedicated to helping small businesses get off the ground, grow and achieve their goals through education and mentorship. They have been doing this for over fifty years. Their website is Score.org]

Before you apply for a loan, you need to think about a variety of questions:

Questions Your Lender Will Ask

- Can the business repay the loan? (Is cash flow greater than debt service?)
- Can you repay the loan if the business fails? (Is collateral sufficient to repay the loan?)
- Does the business collect its bills?
- Does the business pay its bills?
- Does the business control its inventory?
- Does the business control expenses?
- Are the officers committed to the business?
- Does the business have a profitable operating history?
- Does the business match its sources and uses of funds?
- Are sales growing?
- Are profits increasing as a percentage of sales?
- Is there any discretionary cash flow?
- What is the future of the industry?

- Who is your competition and what are their strengths and weaknesses?

Avoid Predatory Lending

It is an unfortunate reality that predatory lending occurs. Predatory lending is lending money to those who really need the money for emergencies, like paying medical bills and repairs, with unfair or abusive tactics and without regard to the borrower's ability to repay that further deepens their money problems. These lenders usually target the poor, minorities, the elderly, and the less educated.

How Predatory Lending Is Practiced:

- **Extreme Interest Rates & Fees.** The lender charges unreasonable interest & fees that the borrower is most likely unable to pay.
- **Stealing Home Equity.** The lender secures their loan with your home equity (home market value above your mortgage amount) with payment terms, interest, and fees that you may not afford to pay back. When you don't make your payments to them, it gives them the right to foreclose on your house to sell it and profit off your home equity, leaving you homeless.
- **Misrepresentation & Hidden Disclosure.** The lender doesn't give the true cost, fees, and terms of the loan.
- *Loan Flipping.* The lender refinances your loan with a new loan that has a higher cost to you.
- **Hidden Balloon Payments.** The attractive low monthly payments can fool the borrower as it is only for a short time. After that, the borrower has to make a big balloon payment to catch up that they cannot afford, which forces them to refinance again.

The best way to avoid predatory lending is to be aware of it and avoid it. Spread the word and protect your family, friends, and loved ones from this. Here are a few tips:

- Work with reputable financial banks, credit unions, and licensed lenders. Don't trust mailers and telephone offers.

- If it seems "too good to be true," it is "too good to be true." Don't gamble with lenders.
- Slow down. If you are being rushed to sign anything, there is a reason for it, so don't do it. Take the contract with you and let them know you will need to review it overnight, and then give it to a person who you trust to read it. You can even ask a banker at your nearest bank to read it and give you their opinion. Bankers can still help you even if you don't have an account with them.
- Question everything. If the lender can't give you an answer that you understand, chances are they don't understand it either. They might be working on commission and want you to sign, sign, and sign so they can get their sales commission quickly.
- No blanks. If there are missing fields or blanks that can be filled in later, don't sign the document yet. You may not know what terms are filled in after you sign the paperwork.

Reducing Debt

There are many ways to reduce your debt balance. These include refinancing the loan, paying down principal, making a call, consolidating, and asking for help.

Refinancing

Interest rates are connected to the overall market economy. When interest rates move lower, consider getting a new loan at the new lower interest rate to pay off current loans with higher interest rates. An example of this occurred after the 2008 mortgage crisis when mortgage rates moved much lower. This gave anyone who recognized it the opportunity to refinance and reduce their monthly mortgage payments and overall total payments. This can be applied to other loans such as student loans and auto loans when you can get a lower interest rate. You may not have to wait until there is a big market change for interest rates to lower; an increase in your credit score might help you qualify for a lower interest rate. Shopping at different banks that can give you a lower interest rate can work in your favor.

Paying Down Principal

The biggest factor in reducing debt is how you schedule your payments. You have two options: Pay Extra or Pay Bi-Weekly (every two weeks)

Paying Extra-10% for example

Let's assume here that you want to reduce your biggest debt, which is your mortgage, but note that you can apply this to other loans as well. Your mortgage is a 30 year, $325,000 loan at 4% interest. The monthly mortgage payment is $1,551.60. Instead of paying that amount, consider paying about 10% extra or about $150 more a month in this example, making your total monthly payment $1,701.60 instead. You will save $40,902.26 in interest payments over the life of the loan by paying more. The calculator to use is an Extra Payment Mortgage Calculator.[72]

$325k Loan: 30 Yr Term @ 4%	Standard	Additional Payment (10%, $150)
Monthly Payment	$1,551.60	$1,701.60
Total Interest Paid	$233,575.90	$192,673.64
Interest Savings		**$40,902.26**

Paying Bi-Weekly (Every Two Weeks)

Use the same mortgage terms listed above. This time, instead of paying extra on your monthly payment, you pay $775.80 every two weeks. It is still the same amount of $1,551.60 monthly. By changing to Bi-Weekly instead of monthly, you save $36,462.60 in interest. The calculator to use is a Bi-Weekly Mortgage Calculator.[73] Here is the result:

$325k Loan: 30 Yr Term @ 4%	Standard Monthly	Bi-Weekly ($775.80)
Monthly Payment :	$1,551.60	$1,551.60 ($775.80 Bi-Weekly)
Total Interest Paid:	$233,575.90	$197,113.30
Interest Savings :		**$36,462.60**

Call & Negotiate

Sometimes, the easiest method is overlooked. Call your debt holder and negotiate a lower interest rate. Additionally, if you have a lump sum of cash that you want to use to pay them off, you can ask for a lower settlement amount. For example, you owe $5,000, and you offer to settle it for $4,000. Asking is powerful.

Consolidate

Instead of having multiple accounts with high interest, consider finding a lender that can consolidate all the debt into one account with a lower interest rate.

Ask For Help

As mentioned in the section on repairing credit, you can consider using a government-approved organization at www.usdoj.gov/ust that can help you lower your debt.

Doing Your Taxes

Paying tax is an important aspect of being a good, responsible citizen. The collective tax dollars are used to build our country and provide many priceless benefits that contribute to our overall well-being. Failure to pay tax or paying them incorrectly can lead to terrible consequences. In this section, I will cover working with a tax professional and tax fundamentals.

Working With A Tax Professional

Certified Public Accountants (CPA), Enrolled Agents (EA), and Licensed Tax Attorneys are the professionals who you can trust to help you with your personal and business taxes. Since they are tax professionals, working with them is an investment on your part. There are pros, cons, and alternatives to using a tax professional.

Pros

- Make it uncomplicated when it gets complicated for you. As life events happen, taxes can be complicated by getting married, having kids, starting a business, investing, or buying a home. Professionals can make your tax calculations easy to understand

and help you maximize any opportunities to save you on your overall tax bill.

- Save time and money. Instead of trying to figure out any possible tax changes and all of your possible deductions, your professional can quickly help you adjust to changes and maximize your tax deductions.
- Double check your work. Even when you can do it yourself, it is wise to have a second look from the perspective of a professional who does it for a living. They may see opportunities and mistakes you overlooked that can make a big difference.

Cons

- It costs you money. It is actually an investment if the professional delivers you value but when they do not, it is a cost. This is why choosing a reputable tax professional like a CPA or an EA that have proven to help others is worth the money to hire them.
- The best may not be available. The best professionals are usually filled up with clients so it is best to plan ahead and work with them as early as you can.
- Tax return preparers aren't required to have professional credentials, so it important to make sure you understand the qualifications of the preparer you select. See the tips below to help you.

Tips for Working with Tax Professionals

- There are many professionals who stand behind their work, and if there are any errors, they will take responsibility for the error and assume the costs of penalties and interest as well as provide IRS audit support if you are audited. Just know that as a taxpayer, you are ultimately responsible for the information reported on your tax return, and you must be the person that pays what is due. However, it is worth the investment to work with the right professionals. Ask upfront what happens when there is an error and how the professional would handle it before you hire them to help you.
- Check on the service fees upfront. The IRS suggests avoiding preparers who base their fee on a percentage of your refund as well as those who say they can get larger refunds than others can.

- Provide records and receipts. The IRS notes that good preparers will ask to see your records and receipts. They'll ask you questions to determine your total income, deductions, tax credits, and other items. Do not rely on a preparer who is willing to e-file your return using your last pay stub instead of your Form W-2. This is against IRS e-file rules.
- Ensure that the preparer signs and includes their PTIN. The IRS says that paid preparers must sign returns and include their PTIN, as required by law. The preparer must also give you a copy of the return.
- Use IRS.gov as your direct tax resource, and report abusive tax preparers and suspected tax fraud to the IRS. Use Form 14157, Complaint: Tax Return Preparer. If you suspect a preparer filed or changed your return without your consent, you should also file Form 14157-A, Return Preparer Fraud or Misconduct Affidavit. You can get these forms at IRS.gov.

Alternatives to Hiring a Professional

- You can use software to help you file your taxes. It will save you money, and it can also save you time.
- Your tax situation should be simple if you elect to use software. If you are using the software but getting confused by many of the questions, then consider working with a professional.
- IRS Free File: do your federal taxes for free. According to IRS.gov, if a person's income is below a certain amount (for example, $64,000 in 2017), he can use the IRS Free File Software.[74] Visit IRS.gov and search for Free File Software. If your income is above the threshold, the IRS.gov website has "Free File Fillable Forms" for you to use.[75]

Tax Fundamentals

Even when working with tax professionals, it is important to know the tax fundamentals so that you can maximize the value of your relationship with them. Here are the fundamentals of tax types, filing taxes, and paying your taxes.

Tax Types

Ordinary Income Tax, Capital Gains Tax, and Real Estate (Property) Tax are the three common taxes that you should be aware of.

Ordinary Income Tax

Ordinary Income Tax is usually tax that does not include long-term capital gains. This tax includes wages, salaries, tips, commissions, bonuses, and other types of compensation from employment, interest, dividends, or net income from businesses. These incomes are taxed at the federal, state, and even some local levels. Depending on your state and local tax rates and cutoffs, you may not be required to pay any tax. Check with your state and local officials as well as ask your tax professional for more updated information. Federal income tax applies to everyone. The U.S. federal income tax is based on the progressive tax system. A progressive tax takes a larger percentage of income from high-income groups than from low-income groups and is based on the concept of ability to pay. A progressive tax system might, for example, tax low-income taxpayers at ten percent, middle-income taxpayers at fifteen percent and high-income taxpayers at thirty percent. Here are the federal income tax brackets for the four types of filers from 2017.

Single Federal Income Tax Bracket, 2017

Rate	Taxable Income Bracket	Tax Owed
10%	$0 to $9,325	10% of Taxable Income ($9,32.50)
15%	$9,325 to $37,950	$932.50 plus 15% of the excess over $9325
25%	$37,950 to $91,900	$5,226.25 plus 25% of the excess over $37,950
28%	$91,900 to $191,650	$18,713.75 plus 28% of the excess over $91,900
33%	$191,650 to $416,700	$46,643.75 plus 33% of the excess over $191,650
35%	$416,700 to $418,400	$120,910.25 plus 35% of the excess over $416,700
39.60%	$418,400+	$121,505.25 plus 39.6% of the excess over $418,400

Head of Household Federal Income Tax Bracket, 2017

Rate	Taxable Income Bracket	Tax Owed
10%	$0 to $13,350	10% of taxable income ($1,335)
15%	$13,350 to $50,800	$1,335 plus 15% of the excess over $13,350
25%	$50,800 to $131,200	$6,952.50 plus 25% of the excess over $50,800
28%	$131,200 to $212,500	$27,052.50 plus 28% of the excess over $131,200
33%	$212,500 to $416,700	$49,816.50 plus 33% of the excess over $212,500
35%	$416,700 to $444,500	$117,202.50 plus 35% of the excess over $416,701
40%	$444,550+	$126,950 plus 39.6% of the excess over $444,550

Married Filing Jointly Federal Income Tax Bracket, 2017

Rate	Taxable Income Bracket	Tax Owed
10%	$0 to $18,650	10% of taxable income ($1,865)
15%	$18,650 to $75,900	$1,865 plus 15% of the excess over $18,650
25%	$75,900 to $153,100	$10,452.50 plus 25% of the excess over $75,900
28%	$153,100 to $233,350	$29,752.50 plus 28% of the excess over $153,100
33%	$233,350 to $416,700	$52,222.50 plus 33% of the excess over $233,350
35%	$416,700 to $470,700	$112,728 plus 35% of the excess over $416,700
40%	$470,700+	$131,628 plus 39.6% of the excess over $470,700

Married Filing Separately Federal Income Tax Bracket, 2017

Rate	Taxable Income Bracket	Tax Owed
10%	$0 to $9,275	10% of taxable income ($9,275)
15%	$9,276 to $37,650	$927.50 plus 15% of the excess over $9,276
25%	$37,651 to $75,950	$5,183.60 plus 25% of the excess over $37,650
28%	$75,951 to $115,725	$14,758.35 plus 28% of the excess over $75,950
33%	$115,726 to $206,675	$25,895.07 plus 33% of the excess over $115,725
35%	$206,676 to $233,475	$55,908.24 plus 35% of the excess over $206,675
40%	$233,476 or more	$65,287.89 plus 39.6% of the excess over $233,475

Notice there are four tables, one for each of the filing statuses: Single, Head of Household, Married Filing Jointly, and Married Filing Separately. Here are the definitions and a tip from the IRS.gov site for each, so you know how it applies to you.[76]

Single

Your filing status is single if you are considered unmarried, and you don't qualify for another filing status.

Head of Household

You may be able to file as head of household if you meet all the following requirements.

- You are unmarried or "considered unmarried" on the last day of the year. See Marital Status, earlier, and Considered Unmarried, later.
- You paid more than half the cost of keeping up a home for the year.
- A qualifying person lived with you in the home for more than half the year (except for temporary absences, such as school). However, if the qualifying person is your dependent parent, he or she doesn't

have to live with you. See Special rule for parent, later, under Qualifying Person.

IRS Tip

If you qualify to file as head of household, your tax rate usually will be lower than the rates for single or married filing separately. You will also receive a higher standard deduction than if you file as single or married filing separately.

Married Filing Jointly

You can choose married filing jointly as your filing status if you are considered married and both you and your spouse agree to file a joint return. On a joint return, you and your spouse report your combined income and deduct your combined allowable expenses. You could file a joint return even if one of you had no income or deductions.

If you and your spouse decide to file a joint return, your tax may be lower than your combined tax for the other filing statuses. Also, your standard deduction (if you don't itemize deductions) may be higher, and you may qualify for tax benefits that don't apply to other filing statuses.

IRS Tip

If you and your spouse each have income, you may want to figure your tax both on a joint return and on separate returns (using the filing status of married filing separately). You can choose the method that gives the two of you the lower combined tax.

Married Filing Separately

You can choose married filing separately as your filing status if you are married. This filing status may benefit you if you want to be responsible only for your own tax or if it results in less tax than filing a joint return.

If you and your spouse don't agree to file a joint return, you must use this filing status unless you qualify for head of household status, discussed later.

You may be able to choose head of household filing status if you are considered unmarried because you live apart from your spouse and meet certain tests (explained later, under Head of Household). This can apply to you even if you aren't divorced or legally separated. If you qualify to file as head of household, instead of as married filing separately, your tax may be lower, you may be able to claim the earned income credit and certain other credits, and your standard deduction will be higher. The head of household filing status allows you to choose the standard deduction even if your spouse chooses to itemize deductions. See Head of Household, later, for more information.

IRS Tip

You will generally pay more combined tax on separate returns than you would on a joint return for the reasons listed under Special Rules, later. However, unless you are required to file separately, you should figure your tax both ways (on a joint return and on separate returns). This way you can make sure you are using the filing status that results in the lowest combined tax. When figuring the combined tax of a married couple, you may want to consider state taxes as well as federal taxes.

Key Tax Terms & Tax Deductions

- **Adjusted Gross Income (AGI):** The IRS defines this as gross income minus adjustments to income. Take your total wages, interest, dividends and short-term capital gains and subtract items such as contributions to a qualified retirement plan and applicable business expenses. Your AGI is the amount on which your tax is based.
- **Earned Income Tax Credit, (EITC or EIC).** The IRS defines EITC as a benefit for working people with low to moderate income. To qualify, you must meet certain requirements and file a tax return, even if you do not owe any tax or are not required to file. EITC reduces the amount of tax you owe and may give you a refund.[77]
- **Standard Deduction.** The IRS defines this as a specific dollar amount that reduces the amount of income on which you're taxed. Your standard deduction consists of the sum of the basic standard deduction and any additional standard deductions for age and/or blindness. In general, the standard deduction

is adjusted each year for inflation and varies according to your filing status, whether you're 65 or older and/or blind, and whether another taxpayer can claim you as a dependent. The standard deduction isn't available to certain taxpayers. You can't take the standard deduction if you itemize your deductions.

The standard deduction amount varies depending on your income, age, and filing status and changes each year. For example, the basic standard deduction for 2016 depends on the filing status. If the taxpayer is:

- Single-$6,300
- Married Filing Jointly-$12,600
- Head of Household-$9,300
- Married Filing Separately-$6,300
- Qualifying Widow(er)-$12,600

Certain taxpayers can't use the standard deduction:[78]

- A married individual filing as married filing separately whose spouse itemizes deductions.
- An individual who files a tax return for a period of fewer than 12 months because of a change in his or her annual accounting period.
- An individual who was a nonresident alien or a dual-status alien during the year. However, nonresident aliens who are married to a U.S. citizen or resident alien at the end of the year and who choose to be treated as U.S. residents for tax purposes can take the standard deduction.

Itemized Deductions. According to the IRS, you should itemize deductions if your allowable itemized deductions are greater than your standard deduction or if you must itemize deductions because you can't use the standard deduction.[79]

You may be able to reduce your tax by itemizing deductions on Form 1040, Schedule A, Itemized Deductions. These may include expenses such as:[80]

- Home mortgage interest
- State and local income taxes or sales taxes (but not both)
- Real estate and personal property taxes
- Gifts to charities
- Casualty or theft losses
- Unreimbursed medical expenses
- Unreimbursed employee business expenses

You would usually benefit by itemizing on Form 1040, Schedule A, if you:[81]

- Can't use the standard deduction or the amount you can claim is limited
- Had large uninsured medical and dental expenses
- Paid interest or taxes on your home
- Had large unreimbursed employee business expenses or other miscellaneous deductions
- Had large uninsured casualty or theft losses, or
- Made large contributions to qualified charities

Your itemized deductions may be limited, and your total itemized deductions may be phased out (reduced) if your adjusted gross income for 2016 exceeds the following threshold amounts for your filing status:

- Single-$259,400
- Married filing jointly or qualifying widow(er)-$311,300
- Married filing separately-$155,650
- Head of household-$285,350

For any more terms, abbreviations, and language that you need explanation and examples for when doing your taxes, please visit IRS. gov or ask your tax professional to help you.

Capital Gains Tax

In Chapter 6, you were introduced to capital gains tax as it applies to investments. Below is detailed information on capital gains and losses provided by the IRS.gov.[82]

According to the IRS, almost everything you own and use for personal or investment purposes is a capital asset. Examples include a home, personal-use items like household furnishings, and stocks or bonds held as investments. When you sell a capital asset, the difference between the adjusted basis (cost) in the asset and the amount you realized from the sale is a capital gain or a capital loss.

You have a capital gain if you sell the asset for more than your adjusted basis. You have a capital loss if you sell the asset for less than your adjusted basis. Losses from the sale of personal-use property, such as your home or car, aren't tax deductible.

Capital gains and losses are classified as long-term or short-term. If you hold the asset for more than one year before you dispose of it, your capital gain or loss is long-term. If you hold it one year or less, your capital gain or loss is short-term. To determine how long you held the asset, count from the day after the day you acquired the asset up to and including the day you disposed of the asset. It is important to note that net short-term capital gains are subject to taxation as ordinary income at graduated tax rates (discussed above "ordinary income tax.").

If you have a net capital gain, a lower tax rate may apply to the gain than the tax rate that applies to your ordinary income. The term "net capital gain" means the amount by which your net long-term capital gain for the year is more than your net short-term capital loss for the year. The term "net long-term capital gain" means long-term capital gains reduced by long-term capital losses including any unused long-term capital loss carried over from previous years.

The tax rate on most net capital gain is no higher than 15% for most taxpayers. Some or all net capital gain may be taxed at 0% if you're in the 10% or 15% ordinary income tax brackets. However, a 20% tax rate on net capital gain applies to the extent that a taxpayer's taxable income exceeds the thresholds set for the ordinary tax rate.

There are a few other exceptions where capital gains may be taxed at rates greater than 15%:

- The taxable part of a gain from selling section 1202 qualified small business stock is taxed at a maximum 28% rate.
- Net capital gains from selling collectibles (such as coins or art) are taxed at a maximum 28% rate.
- The portion of any unrecaptured section 1250 gain from selling section 1250 real property is taxed at a maximum 25% rate.

Real Estate Tax & Deductions

The following Real Estate Tax and Deduction information are from IRS. gov: Please refer to their website for the most up to date information on your specific tax needs.[83]

Real Estate Taxes

Most state and local governments charge an annual tax on the value of real property. This is called a real estate tax. You can deduct the tax if it is assessed uniformly at a like rate on all real property throughout the community. The proceeds must be for general community or governmental purposes and not be a payment for a special privilege granted or service rendered to you.

Deductible Real Estate Taxes

You can deduct real estate taxes imposed on you. You must have paid them either at settlement or closing, or to a taxing authority (either directly or through an escrow account) during the year.

Where to deduct real estate taxes.   Enter the amount of your deductible real estate taxes on Schedule A (Form 1040), line 6.

Real estate taxes paid at settlement or closing.   Real estate taxes are generally divided so that you and the seller each pay taxes for the part of the property tax year you owned the home. Your share of these taxes is fully deductible if you itemize your deductions.

Division of real estate taxes.   For federal income tax purposes, the seller is treated as paying the property taxes up to, but not including, the date of sale. You (the buyer) are treated as paying the taxes beginning with the date of sale. This applies regardless of the lien dates under local law. Generally, this information is included on the settlement statement you get at closing.

You and the seller each are considered to have paid your own share of the taxes, even if one or the other paid the entire amount. You each can deduct your own share, if you itemize deductions, for the year the property is sold.

Example.

You bought your home on September 1. The property tax year (the period to which the tax relates) in your area is the calendar year. The tax for the year was $730 and was due and paid by the seller on August 15.

You owned your new home during the property tax year for 122 days (September 1 to December 31, including your date of purchase). You figure your deduction for real estate taxes on your home as follows.

1.	Enter the total real estate taxes for the real property tax year	$730
2.	Enter the number of days in the property tax year that you owned the property	122
3.	Divide line 2 by 366	.3333
4.	Multiply line 1 by line 3. This is your deduction. Enter it on Schedule A (Form 1040), line 6	$243

Note: You can deduct $243 on your return for the year if you itemize your deductions. You are considered to have paid this amount and can deduct it on your return even if, under the contract, you did not have to reimburse the seller.

- **Delinquent taxes.** Delinquent taxes are unpaid taxes that were imposed on the seller for an earlier tax year. If you agree to pay delinquent taxes when you buy your home, you cannot deduct them. You treat them as part of the cost of your home. See Real estate taxes, later, under Basis.
- **Escrow accounts.** Many monthly house payments include an amount placed in escrow (put in the care of a third party) for real estate taxes. You may not be able to deduct the total you pay into the escrow account. You can deduct only the real estate taxes that the lender actually paid from escrow to the taxing authority. Your real estate tax bill will show this amount.
- **Refund or rebate of real estate taxes.** If you receive a refund or rebate of real estate taxes this year for amounts you paid this year, you must reduce your real estate tax deduction by the amount refunded to you. If the refund or rebate was for real estate taxes paid for a prior year, you may have to include some or all of the refund in your income. For more information, see Recoveries in Pub. 525, Taxable and Nontaxable Income.

Items You Cannot Deduct as Real Estate Taxes

Charges for services are not deductible as real estate taxes. An itemized charge for services to specific property or people is not a tax, even if the charge is paid to the taxing authority. You cannot deduct the charge as a real estate tax if it is:

- A unit fee for the delivery of a service (such as a $5 fee charged for every 1,000 gallons of water you use),
- A periodic charge for a residential service (such as a $20 per month or $240 annual fee charged for trash collection), or
- A flat fee charged for a single service provided by your local government (such as a $30 charge for mowing your lawn because it had grown higher than permitted under a local ordinance).

Filing Your Tax

The main deadline to file your taxes by is mid-April of every year. The date may differ when filing businesses taxes, so check IRS.gov or your tax professional.

When filing your taxes, you have a few options.

- Explore electronic filing options which include IRS Free File, commercial software, and Authorized e-file Providers
- Find a mailing address for paper returns
- Get free tax preparation help
- Choose a tax professional

Exploring Electronic Filing Options

- **Free File:** As mentioned earlier if your income is below $64,000 you can use the Free File at IRS.gov. If it is above that threshold, you can access the Free Fill Fillable Forms instead.
- **Commercial Software:** The IRS allows you to use commercial tax prep software to file your taxes electronically. The software uses a question and answer format that makes doing taxes easier. You must sign your e-filed return electronically.

- **Authorized e-file Providers.** For your convenience, the IRS provides an online database for all Authorized IRS e-file Providers that choose to be included in the database. You can locate the closest Authorized IRS e-file Providers in your area where you can electronically file your tax return. You can access the database on IRS.gov.

Find a Mailing Address for Paper Returns

You can visit IRS.gov to find the mailing address as well as forms to download and print. To avoid errors and file your taxes more quickly, consider using electronic options instead of doing a paper return.

Get Free Tax Prep Help[84]

According to IRS.gov, the Volunteer Income Tax Assistance (VITA) program offers free tax help to people who generally make $54,000 or less, persons with disabilities, and limited English speaking taxpayers who need assistance in preparing their own tax returns. IRS-certified volunteers provide free basic income tax return preparation with electronic filing to qualified individuals.

In addition to VITA, the Tax Counseling for the Elderly (TCE) program offers free tax help for all taxpayers, particularly those who are 60 years of age and older, specializing in questions about pensions and retirement-related issues unique to seniors. The IRS-certified volunteers who provide tax counseling are often retired individuals associated with non-profit organizations that receive grants from the IRS.

VITA and TCE sites are generally located at community and neighborhood centers, libraries, schools, shopping malls and other convenient locations across the country. To locate the nearest VITA or TCE site near you, use the VITA Locator Tool or call 800-906-9887. When looking for a TCE site keep in mind that a majority of the TCE sites are operated by the AARP Foundation's Tax Aide program. To locate the nearest AARP TCE Tax-Aide site between January and April use the AARP Site Locator Tool or call 888-227-7669.

Choose a Tax Professional

As discussed earlier in this chapter, you can work with a tax professional who can help you with tax planning as well as filing your tax. If you don't know anyone that you can trust, you can use the free "Directory of Federal Tax Return Preparers with Credentials and Select Qualifications" on IRS.gov to select a tax professional. The website direct link is https://irs.treasury.gov/rpo/rpo.jsf

Paying your tax

The IRS offers a few methods for you to pay your taxes. This information is provided by IRS.gov. IRS tax payment options are:[85]

- **Pay Online Directly from Your Bank Account.** If you're an individual taxpayer, IRS Direct Pay offers you a free, secure electronic payment method. You can use this by visiting IRS. gov. Use this secure service to pay your taxes for Form 1040 series, estimated taxes or other associated forms directly from your checking or savings account at no cost to you.

- **Pay with Your Debit or Credit Card.** Choose an approved payment processor to make a secure tax payment online or by phone. You can use this option by visiting IRS.gov. You can pay by internet, phone, or mobile device whether you e-file, paper file or are responding to a bill or notice. It's safe and secure- the IRS uses standard service providers and business/commercial card networks, and your information is used solely to process your payment.

Other Ways You Can Pay

The IRS gives you even more options to pay:

1) **Electronic Federal Tax Payment System** (Best Option For Businesses Or Large Payments; Enrollment Required).

The Easiest Way to Pay All Your Federal Taxes (EFTPS®) is a system for paying federal taxes electronically using the Internet, or by phone using the EFTPS® Voice Response System. EFTPS® is offered free by the U.S. Department of Treasury.

2) Electronic Funds Withdrawal (during e-filing).

Electronic Funds Withdrawal (EFW) is an integrated e-file/e-pay option offered only when filing your federal taxes using tax preparation software or through a tax professional. Using this payment option, you may submit one or more payment requests for direct debit from your designated bank account.

3) Same-day wire (bank fees may apply).

You may be able to do a same-day wire from your Financial Institution. Contact your Financial Institution for availability, cost, and cut-off times.

4) Check or money order.

If you choose to mail your tax payment. Make your check, money order or cashier's check payable to U.S. Treasury. Please note:

- Do not send cash through the mail. Enter the amount using all numbers ($###. ##).
- Do not use staples or paper clips to affix your payment to your voucher or return.
- Make sure your check or money order includes the following information:
  - o Your name and address
  - o Daytime phone number
  - o Social Security number (the primary SSN shown first if it's a joint return) or employer identification number
  - o Tax year
  - o Related tax form or notice number
- Mail your payment to the address listed on the notice or instructions, or visit IRS.gov for more information.
- IRS can't accept single check or money order amounts of $100 million or more. You can submit multiple payments or make a same-day wire payment.

5) Cash (at a retail partner).

The quickest, easiest way to make a tax payment is online. If you prefer to pay in cash, the IRS offers a way for you to pay your taxes at a participating retail store. It generally takes five to seven business days to process your payment. Be sure to plan ahead of your due date to ensure your payment is posted timely.

- Step 1. Visit the Official Payments site (http://www.officialpayments. com/fed) and follow the instructions to make cash payment with PayNearMe.

- Step 2. You'll receive an email from Official Payments confirming your information. The IRS will then verify your information. This process may take two to three days.

- Step 3. After the IRS verifies your information, PayNearMe will then send you an email with a link to your payment code and instructions. Either print the payment code at home or send it to your smart phone.

- Final step. Go to the retail store listed in the PayNearMe email and ask the clerk to scan or enter your payment code. You will receive a receipt from the store after they accept your cash. This receipt is confirmation of your payment and should be kept for your records. It usually takes two business days for your payment to post to your account.

Can't Pay Now? You Got Options Too!

The IRS has these options to help you when you cannot pay your income taxes:

- Meet your tax obligation in monthly installments by applying for an online payment agreement.
- Find out if you qualify for an offer in compromise – a way to settle your tax debt for less than the full amount.
- Request to temporarily delay collection until your financial situation improves.

- Visit IRS.gov for details.

Prevent Future Tax Liabilities

If you want to reduce or even eliminate a balance due after filing, you can do so by adjusting your withholding amount or making estimated payments. The IRS Withholding Calculator can help you adjust the amount withheld from your pay by your employer, in order to reduce or eliminate your balance due.[86] Estimated tax is the method you use to pay tax on income that is not subject to withholding, such as self-employment income. Please refer to the resources at IRS.gov for all your specific tax needs.

Chapter Eight
IT'S GAME TIME!

"You don't have to be great to get started, but you have to get started to be great." – Les Brown

WE'VE COME A LONG WAY. If I have fulfilled my mission here to provide you with the financial foundation for your life's successes, then I hope you felt inspired and guided to take control of your financial life and future. If you are a student reading this or someone questioning which career path to take, with the Money Smarts you have learned, you are now ready to freely follow your heart and passion to pursue any career that truly honors and brings out the best in you without worrying about how you can also create financial wealth for yourself following that path. Remember...

It's not *how much* money you make but *how you make* your money that determines your financial freedom.

Choose the career that uplifts you, inspires you, challenges you and that you can really enjoy doing. Regardless of how much the starting pay is, you now know how to increase your earning power and create additional income streams that won't depend on you working to achieve your financial freedom. You are your greatest asset, so don't settle for less and discount yourself. Believe in your skills, talent, and passion. Life only has a play button, no rewind button, so choose to give yourself the opportunity to be the best version of you. You can have your cake and eat it too. You can pursue doing what you love and build wealth with it.

You can do this! It's game time and you don't need to bench yourself. You have the money playbook here with the strategies and the best practices to win. You have what it takes to increase your Earning Power to earn more money. You are in control of your life and in control of your emotions. You can delay your gratification to save more money. You know how and what to invest in to earn money without having to work. You also know the difference between good and bad debt. Bad debt forces you to work for it while good debt works for you.

You've got this. You are going to win. It's just a question of when you will start. So go start now!

If you have read this far, then you know more about money and have more Money Smarts than I did when I began. I have earned millions of dollars with these Money Smarts and helped others do it too. I am excited to hear what you will do with it all. You have a solid foundation and a huge head start on the next generation of success stories. In fact, you probably know more now than most people today, because until now, few people have shared their Money Smarts. If you run into any student or anyone who is hungry for financial growth on your exciting journey, please share this book with them or help them. We all need to help and honor each other, especially our students and graduates who are filled with energy and optimism. Let's keep their bright flame burning.

I don't know why you are reading my words at this moment, but I feel honored that you have given me the opportunity to share what I have learned with you. I am still learning. We never stop learning. I just want to thank you and let you know that it has been amazing to write this book for you and our community.

After working with thousands of students, graduates, and parents worldwide, I do have a good idea as to why you might have landed on this page and found my message at this point in your life. I believe you are here because deep within you, there has been a desire to become more, do more, and achieve more for yourself, family, and loved ones. Perhaps you picked up this book because you decided to become financially independent and take control of your financial life to live more fully with financial freedom. Or perhaps you are already financially successful, and you are looking for new ideas and strategies to further advance your level of success.

Regardless, I believe the fact that you are here has something profoundly to do with your financial goals in life. If that is true, I'd like to share one more story before finishing our conversation here.

Meet Thy

Thy was my student, but I ended up being her client. When I graduated college, I continued my businesses and investments, but I had more free time. With the extra personal time, I wanted to contribute so I began coaching, training, and speaking. I spoke at my alma mater, colleges, high schools, and conventions, and I led training and workshops on various topics including entrepreneurship, motivation, and financial literacy. Along the way, students began to contact me to be mentored and coached, so I did as much as could with the personal time I had. Among the first students I coached was Thy.

Thy had just immigrated to America with her family and spoke little to no English. Her parents had just been hired as minimum wage factory workers, and she had started community college with two younger siblings still in grade school. She had no real job and no money. Furthermore, she needed to take care of her siblings while her parents worked all day.

When I began coaching her, I asked for her goals, and like many students, she didn't have the confidence to set or share her goals. I shared with her that not having goals is like driving without a destination, leading to wasted time and opportunity cost. After she had understood, she began to set and share her goals with me. At first, many of her goals were short-term and too easy to achieve. I then shared with her that she also needed to set goals that would challenge and inspire her. Only goals that are challenging will inspire the necessary changes. The saying goes, "if it doesn't challenge you, it won't change you." After some thought, she was about to share a goal but then stopped and said, "No, I don't think...." At that moment, I had to hear it, because it could be the goal that was challenging enough to get her going.

I finally got her to share. She, very softly, said that her goal was to buy a house for her family. She wanted that American Dream for her family. My response, "That's awesome!" She wasn't expecting such excitement from me, but I then told her not only could she do it, but she could also do it very quickly. Depending on her commitment to personal development, she would be able to buy a house within a few years even while going to school full time.

When I got started, I told myself that the only limits I have are the limits I set for myself so I told her not to set any limits for herself either. She agreed. I then asked her how badly she wanted to achieve this goal. Her eyes lit up, and she said, "I love my family and I absolutely want the best for them... let's do this!" She then shared many personal motivations which I could feel how much she wanted it out of love for her family. From there, I focused on coaching her to achieve this goal.

As the first step, I had her share this goal with her parents and siblings so that, as a family, they understood that they would need to manage their expenses to maximize their savings. I explained to her that she would need to save money for the down payment in order to get a mortgage at a good rate.

For the second step, I had her begin building her credit history so she would have a credit score (FICO score) for lenders to review when she applied for a mortgage. She visited her local bank to open a credit card but was denied. She had no history, so no bank she applied to approved her. Thus, she asked me, and I advised her to open a secured credit card. Within six months of opening the secured line, she was offered an unsecured credit card and continued to build her credit using the practices you already know by now.

Step three, she needed income so needed to increase her earning power. I recommended books for her to gain knowledge and discussed with her the skills she needed to develop. Since she was a full-time student and her English was limited, she didn't have many options for regular time-based employment, so she had to rely on performance-based income and became an independent contractor. She researched diligently, and over time, she was able to earn money by contracting with her local TV stations to help with their shows and contracting with other small businesses to do their bookkeeping.

After two years, she followed up with me about her progress and shared with me some amazing news. She had shared her goal not only with her family but also to some of her older classmates at her community college. One classmate told Thy about a government housing program advertised on the radio that provided local residents with housing down payment assistance. Thy got online and did some research, got on the phone, called the city, and off she went to meet the people in charge of the program. She was the first one there, and she was the youngest as well. Because not only is she still learning English but also the terminology used during the presentation was specific to home buying, she couldn't understand everything that was said.

She attended the same meeting a few times and stayed behind afterward to ask questions. Everywhere she went, she brought her English translation dictionary around. Unfortunately, by the time she applied, the funding was gone. It was on a first-come, first-served basis.

Being persistent, she followed up with the program coordinators and asked about similar opportunities. By this point, they were very familiar with Thy and were also impressed by her persistence. They shared with her information on upcoming opportunities. As they all expected, Thy was first to show up when another funding program began, and this time, she applied immediately. The amount of assistance was $40,000.

She and her family had saved $20,000 already, so the $40,000 down payment assistance program would give her a total of $60,000. As you learned about mortgages, lenders want borrowers to have a 20% down payment and they would prefer to lend the remaining 80% of the purchase price. That meant Thy's family could borrow up to $240,000, and with the current mortgage rate at that time around 4%, the mortgage payment per month was about the same as her rental payments. It made absolute sense for them to buy.

Thy quickly found a lender to pre-approve her. But her credit score wasn't high enough to qualify her for low mortgage rates. She called me for advice, and I shared with her tips on how credit scores are calculated and steps she could take to improve her score. I advised her to get her free credit report and to call each company in the history to ask how it could be improved. After just a few weeks, her credit scores increased and her mortgage lender pre-approved her at a lower mortgage interest rate.

With the $60,000 potential down payment and $240,000 potential mortgage, Thy knew her target price for buying the house was $300,000. She told me later that it wasn't easy finding the right house at that price. It took months, but patience and persistence finally led them to the perfect house. Now the real work began, getting all the parties involved to close the deal. It was complicated. In fact, it was so complicated that the original lender who had pre-approved Thy for a mortgage backed out and denied it. They were unfamiliar with the government down payment program and saw Thy as too high of a risk to lend to. Usually, the buyer is expected to complete all the paperwork and financing to close the deal within six weeks. At this point, the six weeks had already passed, and Thy still had no bank willing to offer the mortgage with the special down payment arrangement she had.

Fortunately, Thy was working directly with the listing agent who represented the seller and also Thy as the buyer. She was very kind and supportive of helping Thy with her goal to buy this house for her family. The agent asked Thy if she expected to get financing soon because she needed to be fair to the seller and find a qualified buyer. Thy asked the agent for another six weeks. The agent promised to try to get permission from the seller but cautioned that it wouldn't be easy.

It appeared that almost everyone Thy worked with was quietly cheering her on because she was a student who was only twenty-one years old and trying to do everything she could to help her family. She was open about her goal, and people wanted to do everything they could to help her achieve it.

After anxiously waiting for a few days, the agent shared with Thy somewhat good news.

The seller agreed to extend the deal period for another six weeks; however, her $5,000 deposit would be non-refundable. This meant that if Thy couldn't find another lender in six weeks, she would lose the $5,000. That was a lot of money and took a very long time to save up.

I remember Thy calling me to ask me what she should do. I couldn't advise her, as that was a decision for her and her family to make since it was their money they were risking. However, I did remind her that this was about faith and belief in herself and her goals. I asked her, how much did she believe, and how strong was her faith?

She and her family decided to believe and had faith. Thy signed the nonrefundable extension agreement and the pressure was on. Thy ended failing her college class that semester because she kept walking out of class to take phone calls. The cost of this deal was getting higher and higher.

With only a few weeks left to the deadline, one bank was open for consideration, but they were the only one interested. Thy had no other option but to make the best of this. This bank needed Thy to provide two years of tax returns. Not good...

Thy didn't have two years of tax returns at that time. This is not going to work for the bank. Another dead end. She was running out of time.

Thy immediately called the bank and discussed her situation and asked for other possible options. The bank discussed with Thy a possible exception, employment strength verification, which included an employer letter and a college degree check. The lender wanted to check the degree and the employment to see if they were related. If they were, it would indicate greater employment stability and strength to qualify under the exception to the two-year tax return requirement.

Thy contacted her college counselor to help her verify with the bank that she was pursuing her degree in Accounting, and then she contacted her recent employer who hired her as an accountant. This was about a two-week process, so it was the last hope for Thy and her family.

Thy said she wasn't sure how things would turn out but told me that if it didn't work out, she would still be proud of herself because she did everything she could think of. I agreed with her that most people regret what they don't do more than they regret what they did. Thy and her family prepared for the worst as they waited for the response.

The bank came back and said they now needed to do a home inspection. "Is that good news?" Thy asked me. I said, "Yes! That means the bank is accepting your application to move forward, and they are now inspecting the house to make sure it is a property that they can use as security for the mortgage. As long as the property is worth $300,000 or more, then the lender will lend the 80% as agreed." Only about one week was left before time was up, and the seller was getting impatient. The agent told Thy that the seller was prepared to allow other buyers to make offers so that after the week was up, they could begin working with other buyers.

The bank came back with the results of the inspection. Unfortunately, it was not good news. The inspection showed the property did not have three bedrooms as described. One of the rooms didn't have a closet, so it could not be considered a bedroom. The bank would not lend Thy the money based on that.

This came out of nowhere. Thy and the agent could not believe that after all the hard work, the deal fell apart because of a missing closet. Thy couldn't accept that decision, nor could the agent. After some discussion, the bank did allow Thy to add a closet; according to the Bank's requirement, if a closet was added, they could move forward with the mortgage.

A closet was put in right away. The bank came back and completed another property inspection. If it fails again, the deal is gone.

On the last day, the agent called Thy and said, "Thy, the bank just spoke with me and the house is yours. Congratulations." Thy couldn't believe it. When they told me the news, I teared up. I was so proud. Her parents couldn't believe it either; they were planning for the worst, and they all thanked God for everything.

Thy and her family invited me over for dinner to thank me. Afterward, Thy called me to say, "Thanks for seeing more in me than I saw in myself and for believing in me more than I believed in myself."

As a bonus, because they owned the house, after five years, the house has appreciated over $250,000 above what they bought it for. In order for her parents to save that same amount, it would not be possible in their lifetime with their current age and earning a minimum wage. But through the investment in owning their house, it became real.

Henry Ford said, "Whether you think you can, or you think you can't – you're right." Thy, against all the odds, bought a house for her family at age 21 while still going to community college and taking English language development classes. She had not only to overcome her self-doubts but also the doubts of many others who said she couldn't do it. Sometimes, in our lives, it is the closest people to us that may accidentally hurt us by telling us to not reach for a goal out of the good intentions of protecting us from failure. Thy believed she could buy a house for her family, and she did it. Success is a personal responsibility; don't blame or depend on others. Thy's first challenge was herself. She had to first win the fight with her mind to become mentally stronger and think more independently to stop allowing the negativity of others to affect her mind. Emotionally, she had to guard herself to prevent how others felt from affecting her motivation to keep going. Every time she hit a wall, she climbed over it, believing she would find a path beyond it. She believed she could, and she was right. How many other people can do it but think they can't? Believe you can, and you will be right too.

Thy soon finished college, and after some time, my business grew, and I needed someone who could really customize an accounting system that could meet my demands. I had tried many accounting firms and CFOs, but they could never meet my needs. I thought of Thy, as she had proved to me that she was not only hardworking but was also a very persistent person who could rise to any challenge. I contacted her, and I became one of her accounting clients. That's how I became the client of Thy, who was once my student. Even to this day, I am inspired by her actions and honored to be part of her story.

I hope that in writing this *Money Smarts* book, I have become part of your story too. I hope that I have inspired you to believe in yourself more so that you can set more goals to become more and achieve more for yourself, family, and loved ones. Along your journey, I also hope that you can further share with others and help others achieve their goals too. Let's also cheer on the students and people you know that may have been overlooked or not given many opportunities. Help them find their confidence and share with them the knowledge to believe in what's possible for them.

Interested in Mastering Your Money Skills and Playing the Game of Money for Real Results?

Before writing this book, I had a different approach to helping students learn Money Smarts. Instead of writing this book, I spent years creating the "Money Smarts: Mastering Your Money Skills" board game to help students learn and develop their money skills in a lifelike simulation with real money rules and strategies to apply. Only the player who truly possesses Money Smarts and skills will win the board game. Even if a player can win it once, unless that player can adapt and apply different Money Smarts, that player may not be able to win it again easily.

The belief I had when creating the board game was that while you could learn all the financial strategies in the world, you wouldn't have any results until you could turn that money knowledge into a skill that you could apply and get results. My approach to coaching is that my students need results and skills to prove that they are truly prepared to succeed in life. This board game did just that for me, and it has changed many of my student's lives.

I didn't think this game could be made available to others, even though many asked for it because it would require a lot of one-on-one time to coach the student on the Money Smarts before they could effectively play the game.

This was why this book, *Money Smarts,* was written, in response to many requests from students, parents, financial professionals, and educators, who have played the game with me and seen the life changing results, but believed it was missing this book to serve as the critical course for money knowledge. You have this book now. This book is your money game playbook not only to win the board game but to win in life.

If you are interested in learning more about the opportunity to practice your Money Smarts, please visit MoneySmarts.com and click on Board Game link.

Thank you once again for allowing me to be part of your journey to success. I look forward to continuing our conversation in another capacity. We might even have the chance to sit down and play the Money Smarts board game together!

Until then, dream big dreams and take big actions. -Nathan

ACKNOWLEDGEMENTS

FROM START TO END, THANK you God, all is made possible by your blessings.

To my parents who are my heroes. How you live and the actions you take in life are extraordinary. I'm truly blessed to be your son. I can never thank you enough for all of your sacrifices, patience, and love. Helen, Philip, Stacey, Steven, Jessie, Donna, Christopher, John and Michelle, I am the luckiest little brother to have such great love from you. Thank you all.

To my wife, Thy, you are the love and rock of my life. Thank you for always believing in me and standing with me without hesitation through all the challenges. You are such a great mother and our family is so blessed to have you be the heart of it all. Our daughters and I love you so much.

To my nieces, nephews, and extended family thank you for your love and support. My journey isn't complete without you.

To Brian Lam who believed in me, guided me, and coached me to do what I do today. If it weren't for your mentorship and friendship, I wouldn't be where I am.

To Youth Leadership America (YLA) students, I couldn't have done this without you. You have been my inspiration and drive. Thank you for always raising the bar so I can become better to serve.

To Mark Victor Hansen and the Horatio Alger Association, thank you for giving me the opportunity to succeed with your scholarship, mentorship, and friendship. My entrepreneurial journey wouldn't have been possible without you.

To my community mentors and advisors, thank you for all of your guidance and support throughout my high school, college, and professional life. It's not possible to name you all but I want you to know how deeply appreciative I am to have you in my life. You inspire and influence me more than you would ever know.

To the Anaheim Family YMCA and its board of directors, thank you for changing my life. It was through your program that helped me find my voice and confidence in high school. Thank you for believing in me and allowing me to be a part of such a life changing organization.

To Linda Newby who sponsored me when I didn't have the money for the YMCA Youth & Government program. Your act of kindness helped me become the runner up for California Youth Governor and made me believe more in myself.

To Scott Mukri, Chris French, Carolyn Poulos, and Danny Wilcox for being my amazing program advisors who personally invest time to help me grow and discover my potential. Your advisory, support, and friendship have been instrumental in my personal development. Thank you so much for being a part of my life.

To Kiwanis and Key Club, thank you for giving me the platform to serve and learn about servant leadership. I am who I am because of the opportunities made possible by your organization.

To Gary Green, thank you for your guidance, belief, and friendship. I wouldn't be able to start investing without your support.

To Mr. Steven Leptich who taught me 7th-grade math at Brookhurst Jr High, thank you for believing in me more than I believed in myself. Your belief in me changed the course of my life. I cannot thank you enough. Everything that happened after 7th grade is made possible by you. Thank you, Mr. Leptich.

To Laura Sowers who guided me into college. Thank you for support in my transition from high school and being the support I needed to believe in myself to pursue USC.

To Oxford Academy family who not only challenged me academically, but also on my personal growth, thank you! Thank you to all the school administrators, teachers, and friends. You have a profound effect on me and have influenced me more than you know.

To Paul Orfalea, Steven Mednick, Patrick Henry, and Tom O'Malia, who are my entrepreneurial professors at USC, you have taught the art of business and helped me pursue my entrepreneurship journey. Thank you for challenging me and believing in me.

To Chris Odoca and Andrew Hamilton, thank you for your friendship and inspiration. You certainly impacted my life for the better and I am grateful to have you as friends.

To my customers, clients, partners, and students who made everything possible for me. Thank you all. I am only where am because of your support.

To all my supporters, friends, and fans, I appreciate and thank you all! I apologize deeply for not being able to name all of your names or this book would ever end... Please know that I thank you very much!

Nothing is possible without the support of my staff and team members. Thank you for managing the businesses and making it possible for me to have more time to help and mentor students. You are family to me and I appreciate all that you have done. I cannot thank you enough.

Finally, to my current and future students — I am honored to be your instructor, teacher, and mentor. Thank you for allowing me to be a part of your life and success journey. You continue to inspire and motivate me to never give up working hard in what I believe in. Thank You!

ABOUT THE AUTHOR

Nathan Nguyen became a millionaire at age 23 while going to college full time and still successfully graduated from the University of Southern California with his bachelor's degree in business. His success story has been featured in the all-time bestselling Chicken Soup for the Soul series book *Chicken Soup for the Extraordinary Teens Soul* as well as *The Richest Kids in America*.

With his success over the past decade after graduating college, he is now on a mission to spread financial literacy and proficiency across America and the world. While it deals with money, his approach isn't just about dollars and cents. He believes personal finance begins first with personal development. Anyone at any age regardless of any background or adversity can achieve financial success and freedom when they simply commit to becoming more to achieve more.

As a passionate educator, multimillion-dollar serial entrepreneur, and a blessed father, Nathan is enabling the younger generation to dream big dreams and their families but also their communities. He is relentless at studying more effective ways, creating solutions, and inventing tools to help students realize their greater potential and develop key life skills to succeed more in life.

Nathan further commits to being a change agent for the younger generation by being a frequent speaker, guest lecturer, and skills trainer for schools, colleges, universities, and student conventions. To connect with Nathan and join his mission to help students achieve more, please visit www.nathannguyen.com

.

(ENDNOTES)

1   Schenke, J. (2014). Only 1 in 3 college students getting key work experience they need, according to survey. *Purdue University News*. Retrieved from http://purdue.edu/newsroom/releases/2014/Q4/only-1-in-3-college-students-getting-key-work-experience-they-need,-according-to-survey.html

2   Strauss, K. (2016). These Are The Skills Bosses Say New College Grads Do Not Have. *Forbes*. Retrieved from www.forbes.com/sites/karstenstrauss/2016/05/17/these-are-the-skills-bosses-say-new-college-grads-do-not-have/#31cbc1945491

3   Fottrell, Q. (2017). Half of American families are living paycheck to paycheck. *MarketWatch*. Retrieved from http://www.marketwatch.com/story/half-of-americans-are-desperately-living-paycheck-to-paycheck-2017-04-04

4   Morrissey, M. (2016). The State of American Retirement: How 401(k)s have failed most American Workers *Retirement Inequality Chartbook*. Washington, DC: Economic Policy Institute.

5   Larrimore, J., Arthur-Bentil, M., Dodini, S., & Thomas, L. (2015). Report on the Economic Well-Being of U.S. Households in 2014. Washington, DC: Federal Reserve Board.

6   Cowie, W. (2014). An Astounding Number of Americans Aren't Investing A Cent. *Business Insider*. Retrieved from www.businessinsider.com/an-astounding-number-of-americans-arent-investing-a-cent-2014-12

7   Friedman, Z. (2017). Student Loan Debt In 2017: A $1.3 Trillion Crisis. *Forbes*. Retrieved from www.forbes.com/sites/zackfriedman/2017/02/21/student-loan-debt-statistics-2017/#d709d915daba

8   Lanza, A. (2016). Study: Student Loan Borrowers Delaying Other
     Life Decisions. *U.S. News*. Retrieved from www.usnews.com/
     education/blogs/student-loan-ranger/articles/2016-01-20/study-
     student-loan-borrowers-delaying-other-life-decisions

9   Fry, R. (2015). Millennials surpass Gen Xers as the largest
     generation in U.S. labor force. *Fact Tank: News in the Numbers*.
     Retrieved from Pew Research Center website: http://www.
     pewresearch.org/fact-tank/2015/05/11/millennials-surpass-gen-
     xers-as-the-largest-generation-in-u-s-labor-force/

10   Brennan, C. (2017). Millennials earn 20% less than Boomers did
     at same stage of life. *USA Today*. Retrieved from www.usatoday.
     com/story/money/2017/01/13/millennials-falling-behind-boomer-
     parents/96530338/

11   Landsbaum, C. (2015). Millennials Are the Most Educated, Worst
     Paid Generation. *Complex*. Retrieved from http://www.complex.
     com/pop-culture/2015/08/millennials-are-the-most-educated-
     worst-paid-generation

12   Bidwell, A. (2015). Survey: College Students Becoming Less
     Financially Responsible. *U.S. News*. Retrieved from www.usnews.
     com/news/blogs/data-mine/2015/04/02/college-students-
     becoming-less-financially-responsible-study-says

13   Sun, W. (2015). 7 Frightening Millennial Money Trends. *Forbes*.
     Retrieved from www.forbes.com/sites/winniesun/2015/10/30/hallowe
     enmillennials/#1d3db8b04601

14   Sun, W. (2015). 7 Frightening Millennial Money Trends. *Forbes*.
     Retrieved from www.forbes.com/sites/winniesun/2015/10/30/hallowe
     enmillennials/#1d3db8b04601

15   Dickler, J. (2017). Millennials aren't as smart about money as
     they think. *CNBC*. Retrieved from www.cnbc.com/2017/02/14/
     millennials-arent-as-smart-about-money-as-they-think.html

16 Garcia, T. (2016). Starbucks has more customer money on cards than many banks have in deposits. *MarketWatch*. Retrieved from http://www.marketwatch.com/story/starbucks-has-more-customer-money-on-cards-than-many-banks-have-in-deposits-2016-06-09

17 Investopedia. Rule of 72. (2017). *Terms*, from www.investopedia.com/terms/r/ruleof72.asp

18 Holland, K. (2016). One-Third of High Earners Are Living Paycheck to Paycheck. *NBC News*. Retrieved from www.nbcnews.com/business/retirement/one-third-high-earners-are-living-paycheck-paycheck-n342726

19 Merle, A. (2017). The Reading Habits of Ultra-Successful People. *The Blog*. Retrieved from www.huffingtonpost.com/andrew-merle/the-reading-habits-of-ult_b_9688130.html

20 Graduate Management Admission Council. (2017). Corporate Recruiters Survey Report 2017 *Research Insights*. Reston, VA. Retrieved from http://www.gmac.com/~/media/Files/gmac/Research/Employment-Outlook/2017-gmac-corporate-recruiters-web-release.pdf

21 Graduate Management Admission Council. (2016). Corporate Recruiters Survey Report 2017 *Research Insights*. Reston, VA. Retrieved from http://www.gmac.com/~/media/Files/gmac/Research/Employment-Outlook/2016-corporate-recruiters-web-release.pdf

22 Intuit Quickbooks. (2015). Intuit 2020 Report. Mountain View, CA. Retrieved from http://http-download.intuit.com/http.intuit/CMO/intuit/futureofsmallbusiness/intuit_2020_report.pdf

23 List of wealthiest historical figures. (2017). *Wikpiedia*, from en.wikipedia.org/wiki/List_of_wealthiest_historical_figures#Early_modern_to_modern_period. Retrieved from https://en.wikipedia.org/wiki/List_of_wealthiest_historical_figures#Early_modern_to_modern_period

24 Weatherspoon, C. P. (1990). Giant Sequoia. In R. M. Burns & B.
    H. Honkala (Eds.), *Silvics of North America* (Vol. 1). Washington,
    DC: U.S. Department of Agriculture Forest Service. Retrieved
    from https://www.na.fs.fed.us/spfo/pubs/silvics_manual/
    Volume_1/sequoiadendron/giganteum.htm

25 Szalay, J. (2017). Giant Sequoias and Redwoods: The Largest
    and Tallest Trees. *Live Science*. Retrieved from www.livescience.
    com/39461-sequoias-redwood-trees.html

26 Weatherspoon, C. P. (1990). Giant Sequoia. In R. M. Burns
    & B. H. Honkala (Eds.), *Silvics of North America* (Vol. 1).
    Washington, DC: U.S. Department of Agriculture Forest
    Service. Retrieved from https://www.na.fs.fed.us/spfo/pubs/
    silvics_manual/Volume_1/sequoiadendron/giganteum.htm

27 Lanzen, M. (2013). Feeling Our Emotions. *Scientific American*.
    Retrieved from www.scientificamerican.com/article/feeling-our-
    emotions/

28 Hadad, C. (2015). What the 'marshmallow test' can teach
    you about your kids. *CNN*. Retrieved from http://www.cnn.
    com/2014/12/22/us/marshmallow-test/index.html

29 Mischel, W. (2014). The Marshmallow Test: Mastering Self-
    Control. Boston, MA: Little, Brown and Company.

30 Federal Trade Commission. (2014). *Understanding Vehicle Finance*.
    Consumer Information Retrieved from www.consumer.ftc.gov/
    articles/0056-understanding-vehicle-financing.

31 According to the Kaiser Family Foundation (KFF): Backman,
    M. (2017). This Is the No. 1 Reason American File for
    Bankruptcy. *The Motley Fool*. Retrieved from www.fool.com/
    retirement/2017/05/01/this-is-the-no-1-reason-americans-file-for-
    bankrup.aspx

32 United States Census Bureau. (2014). Where is the Wealth?
    - Median Household Net Worth by Quintile. *Infographics*

& *Visualizations*. Retrieved from https://census.gov/library/visualizations/2014/comm/cb14-156_net_worth.html

33 Paul, K. (2017). $1 billion in gift cards go unused every year — here's how to avoid that. *MarketWatch*. Retrieved from http://www.marketwatch.com/story/1-billion-in-gift-cards-go-unused-every-year-heres-how-to-avoid-that-2016-12-30

34 Internal Revenue Service. (2016). *IRS Announces 2017 Pension Plan Limitations; 401(k) Contribution Limit Remains Unchanged at $18,000 for 2017*. Retrieved from www.irs.gov/uac/newsroom/irs-announces-2017-pension-plan-limitations-401k-contribution-limit-remains-unchanged-at-18000-for-2017.

35 Internal Revenue Service. (2017). Traditional and Roth IRAs. Retrieved from https://www.irs.gov/retirement-plans/traditional-and-roth-iras

36 Hoefflinger, M. (2017). Inside Mark Zuckerberg's controversial decision to turn down Yahoo's $1 billion early offer to buy Facebook. *Business Insider*. Retrieved from http://www.businessinsider.com/why-mark-zuckerberg-turned-down-yahoos-1-billion-offer-to-buy-facebook-in-2006-2017-4

37 The Associated Press. (2007). Microsoft Invests $240 Million in Facebook. *NBC News*. Retrieved from www.nbcnews.com/id/21458486/ns/business-us_business/t/microsoft-invests-million-facebook/#.WX4IEojyvIV

38 Oran, O., & Barr, A. (2012). Facebook prices at top of range in landmark IPO. *Reuters*. Retrieved from http://www.reuters.com/article/us-facebook-idUSBRE84G14Q20120517

39 Koba, M. (2012). Facebook's IPO: What We Know Now. Retrieved from www.cnbc.com/id/47043815

40 Ludwig, S. (2012). Mark Zuckerberg Owns 28.2% of Facebook, Peter Thiel has 2.5%. *Venture Beat*. Retrieved from https://venturebeat.com/2012/02/01/facebook-s-1-zuckerberg-ownership/

41   Mac, R. (2012). How Much Facebook's Billionaires Are Worth Now That IPO Has Priced. *Forbes*. Retrieved from www. forbes.com/sites/ryanmac/2012/05/17/how-much-facebooks-billionaires-are-worth-now-that-ipo-has-priced/#7a88a7d6c6cf

42   Porter's five forces analysis. (2017). *Wikipedia*. Retrieved from http://en.wikipedia.org/wiki/Porter%27s_five_forces_analysis

43   PEST analysis. (2017). *Wikipiedia*. Retrieved from http://en.wikipedia.org/wiki/PEST_analysis

44   SWOT analysis. (2017). *Wikpiedia*. Retrieved from http://en.wikipedia.org/wiki/SWOT_analysis

45   Pepitone, J. (2013). Marissa Mayer's biggest Yahoo buy is 75% cool factor. *CNN Tech*. Retrieved from http://money.cnn.com/2013/08/09/technology/yahoo-tumblr-goodwill/index.html

46   Investopedia. Certified Financial Planner. (2017). *Terms*. Retrieved from www.investopedia.com/terms/c/cfp.asp

47   Investopedia. Chartered Financial Analyst - CFA. (2017). *Terms*. Retrieved from www.investopedia.com/terms/c/cfa.asp#ixzz4mh3VSRml

48   Investopedia. Chartered Financial Consultant - ChFC. (2017). *Terms*. Retrieved from www.investopedia.com/terms/c/chartered-financial-consultant-chfc.asp#ixzz4mh3sa3aL

49   Investopedia. Chartered Life Underwriter - CLU. (2017). *Terms*. Retrieved from www.investopedia.com/terms/c/clu.asp#ixzz4mh2Z3oll

50   Investopedia. Registered Investment Advisor - RIA. (2017). *Terms*. Retrieved from www.investopedia.com/terms/r/ria.asp#ixzz4mh4I4D00

51 United States Securities and Exchange Commission. (2017). Stocks. *Introduction to Investing*. Retrieved from https://investor.gov/introduction-investing/basics/investment-products/stocks

52 United States Securities and Exchange Commission. (2017). Bonds. *Introduction to Investing*. Retrieved from https://investor.gov/introduction-investing/basics/investment-products/bonds

53 United States Securities and Exchange Commission. (2017). Mutual Funds. *Introduction to Investing*. Retrieved from https://investor.gov/investing-basics/investment-products/mutual-funds

54 United States Securities and Exchange Commission. (2017). Exchange Traded Funds (ETFs). *Introduction to Investing*. Retrieved from https://investor.gov/introduction-investing/basics/investment-products/exchange-traded-funds-etfs

55 United States Securities and Exchange Commission. (2017). Real Estate Investment Trusts (REITs). *Introduction to Investing*. Retrieved from https://investor.gov/introduction-investing/basics/investment-products/real-estate-investment-trusts-REITs

56 United States Securities and Exchange Commission. (2017). Commodities. *Introduction to Investing*. Retrieved from https://investor.gov/introduction-investing/basics/investment-products/commodities

57 United States Securities and Exchange Commission. (2017). Municipal Bonds. *Introduction to Investing*. Retrieved from https://investor.gov/introduction-investing/basics/investment-products/municipal-bonds

58 Official statements produced before June 1, 2009 and continuing disclosure documents produced before July 1, 2009, may be available from one of the following organizations: Bloomberg Municipal Repository, DPC Data, Interactive Data Pricing and Reference Data or Standard & Poor's. These organizations may charge a fee.

59   FINRA's Market Data Center also offers price and trade
     information at www.finra.org/marketdata .

60   United States Securities and Exchange Commission. (2017).
     Annuities. *Introduction to Investing*. Retrieved from https://
     investor.gov/introduction-investing/basics/investment-products/
     annuities

61   United States Securities and Exchange Commission. (2017).
     Saving For Education - 529 Plans. *Introduction to Investing*.
     Retrieved from https://investor.gov/introduction-investing/
     basics/investment-products/saving-education-529-plans

62   Financial Industry Regulatory Authority. (2016). Smart Saving
     for College–Better Buy Degrees: 529 Plans and Other College
     Savings Options Retrieved from https://www.finra.org/file/
     smart-saving-college

63   Investopedia. Certified Public Accountant - CPA. (2017). *Terms*.
     Retrieved from http://www.investopedia.com/terms/c/cpa.asp

64   Investopedia. Enrolled Agent - EA. (2017). *Terms*. Retrieved
     from http://www.investopedia.com/terms/e/enrolled_agent.asp

65   valueinvestingpro. (2009). Warren Buffet on Ben
     Graham: YouTube. Retrieved from www.youtube.com/
     watch?v=HCZMs01W0KM.
     Also see: Kennon, J. (2016). Warren Buffett Biography and the
     Evolution of Berkshire Hathaway *The Balance*. Retrieved from
     https://www.thebalance.com/warren-buffett-biography-356436

66   California Department of Consumer Affairs. (2017). Know
     Your Score. Retrieved from http://dca.ca.gov/publications/
     knowyourscore.shtml

67   Federal Reserve Bank of St. Louis. (2017). Total Consumer
     Credit Owned and Securitized, Outstanding / Gross Domestic
     Product * 100 *FRED Economic Data*. Retrieved from http://fred.
     stlouisfed.org/graph/?graph_id=128138&category_id=7519#0

68 Consumer Finance Protection Bureau. (2016). What are the
    main differences between federal student loans and private
    student loans? Retrieved from www.consumerfinance.gov/ask-
    cfpb/what-are-the-main-differences-between-federal-student-
    loans-and-private-student-loans-en-545/

69 Federal Reserve Bank of St. Louis. (2017). Total Consumer Credit
    Owned and Securitized, Outstanding / Gross Domestic Product *
    100 *FRED Economic Data*. Retrieved from http://fred.stlouisfed.
    org/graph/?graph_id=128138&category_id=7519#0

70 Federal Reserve Bank of St. Louis. (2017). Total Consumer Credit
    Owned and Securitized, Outstanding / Gross Domestic Product *
    100 *FRED Economic Data*. Retrieved from http://fred.stlouisfed.
    org/graph/?graph_id=128138&category_id=7519#0

71 U.S. Small Business Administration. (2017). Borrowing Money
    for Your Business. *Starting a Business*. Retrieved from www.sba.
    gov/starting-business/business-financials/borrowing-money-your-
    business

72 Mortgage Calculator. (2017). Extra Mortgage Payment Calculator.
    Retrieved from www.mortgagecalculator.org/calculators/what-if-i-
    pay-more-calculator.php

73 Mortgage Calculator. (2017). Retrieved from www.
    mortgagecalculator.org/

74 Internal Revenue Service. (2017). Free File: Do Your Federal Taxes
    for Free. Retrieved from www.irs.gov/uac/free-file-do-your-federal-
    taxes-for-free

75 Internal Revenue Service. (2017). Free File: Do Your Federal Taxes
    for Free. Retrieved from www.irs.gov/uac/free-file-do-your-federal-
    taxes-for-free

76 Internal Revenue Service. (2016). Qualifying Widow(er) with
    Dependent Child. *Filing Status*. Retrieved from www.irs.gov/
    publications/p17/ch02.html#en_US_2016_publink1000170830

77   Internal Revenue Service. (2017). Earned Income Tax Credit (EITC). Retrieved from www.irs.gov/credits-deductions/individuals/earned-income-tax-credit

78   Internal Revenue Service. (2017). Earned Income Tax Credit (EITC). Retrieved from https://www.irs.gov/credits-deductions/individuals/earned-income-tax-credit

79   Internal Revenue Service. (2017). Topic 501 - Should I Itemize? Retrieved from www.irs.gov/taxtopics/tc501.html

80   Internal Revenue Service. (2017). Itemize or Choose the Standard Deduction. Retrieved from www.irs.gov/uac/itemize-or-choose-the-standard-deduction

81   Internal Revenue Service. (2017). Topic 501 - Should I Itemize? Retrieved from www.irs.gov/taxtopics/tc501.html

82   Internal Revenue Service. (2017). Topic 409 - Capital Gains and Losses. Retrieved from www.irs.gov/taxtopics/tc409.html

83   Internal Revenue Service. (2017). Publication 530 - Main Content. Retrieved from www.irs.gov/publications/p530/ar02.html

84   Internal Revenue Service. (2016). Free Tax Return Preparation for Qualifying Taxpayers. Retrieved from www.irs.gov/individuals/free-tax-return-preparation-for-you-by-volunteers

85   Internal Revenue Service. (2017). Payments. Retrieved from www.irs.gov/payments

86   Internal Revenue Service. (2016). IRS Withholding Calculator. Retrieved from https://www.irs.gov/individuals/irs-withholding-calculator

WORKS CITED

BACKMAN, M. (2017). This Is the No. 1 Reason American File for Bankruptcy. *The Motley Fool.* Retrieved from www.fool.com/retirement/2017/05/01/this-is-the-no-1-reason-americans-file-for-bankrup.aspx

BIDWELL, A. (2015). Survey: College Students Becoming Less Financially Responsible. *U.S. News.* Retrieved from www.usnews.com/news/blogs/data-mine/2015/04/02/college-students-becoming-less-financially-responsible-study-says

BRENNAN, C. (2017). Millennials earn 20% less than Boomers did at same stage of life. *USA Today.* Retrieved from www.usatoday.com/story/money/2017/01/13/millennials-falling-behind-boomer-parents/96530338/

CALIFORNIA DEPARTMENT OF CONSUMER AFFAIRS. (2017). Know Your Score. Retrieved from http://dca.ca.gov/publications/knowyourscore.shtml

CONSUMER FINANCE PROTECTION BUREAU. (2016). What are the main differences between federal student loans and private student loans? Retrieved from www.consumerfinance.gov/ask-cfpb/what-are-the-main-differences-between-federal-student-loans-and-private-student-loans-en-545/

COWIE, W. (2014). An Astounding Number of Americans Aren't Investing A Cent. *Business Insider.* Retrieved from www.businessinsider.com/an-astounding-number-of-americans-arent-investing-a-cent-2014-12

DICKLER, J. (2017). Millennials aren't as smart about money as they think. *CNBC.* Retrieved from www.cnbc.com/2017/02/14/millennials-arent-as-smart-about-money-as-they-think.html

FEDERAL RESERVE BANK OF ST. LOUIS. (2017). Total Consumer Credit Owned and Securitized, Outstanding / Gross Domestic Product * 100 FRED Economic Data. Retrieved from http:// fred.stlouisfed.org/graph/?graph_id=128138&category_id=7519#0

FEDERAL TRADE COMMISSION. (2014). Understanding Vehicle Finance. *Consumer Information.* Retrieved from www.consumer.ftc.gov/articles/0056-understanding-vehicle-financing

FINANCIAL INDUSTRY REGULATORY AUTHORITY. (2016). Smart Saving for College–Better Buy Degrees: 529 Plans and Other College Savings Options. Retrieved from www.finra.org/file/smart-saving-college

FOTTRELL, Q. (2017). Half of American families are living paycheck to paycheck. *MarketWatch.* Retrieved from www.marketwatch.com/story/half-of-americans-are-desperately-living-paycheck-to-paycheck-2017-04-04

FRIEDMAN, Z. (2017). Student Loan Debt In 2017: A $1.3 Trillion Crisis. *Forbes.* Retrieved from www.forbes.com/sites/zackfriedman/2017/02/21/student-loan-debt-statistics-2017/#d709d915daba

FRY, R. (2015). Millennials surpass Gen Xers as the largest generation in U.S. labor force. *Fact Tank: News in the Numbers.* Retrieved from Pew Research Center website: www.pewresearch.org/fact-tank/2015/05/11/millennials-surpass-gen-xers-as-the-largest-generation-in-u-s-labor-force/

GARCIA, T. (2016). Starbucks has more customer money on cards than many banks have in deposits. *MarketWatch.* Retrieved from www.marketwatch.com/story/starbucks-has-more-customer-money-on-cards-than-many-banks-have-in-deposits-2016-06-09

GRADUATE MANAGEMENT ADMISSION COUNCIL. (2016). The Corporate Recruiters Survey Report 2016 Research Insights. Reston, VA.

GRADUATE MANAGEMENT ADMISSION COUNCIL. (2017). The Corporate Recruiters Survey Report 2017 Research Insights. Reston, VA.

HADAD, C. (2015). What the 'marshmallow test' can teach you about your kids. *CNN*. Retrieved from www.cnn.com/2014/12/22/us/marshmallow-test/index.html

HOEFFLINGER, M. (2017). Inside Mark Zuckerberg's controversial decision to turn down Yahoo's $1 billion early offer to buy Facebook. *Business Insider*. Retrieved from www.businessinsider.com/why-mark-zuckerberg-turned-down-yahoos-1-billion-offer-to-buy-facebook-in-2006-2017-4

HOLLAND, K. (2016). One-Third of High Earners Are Living Paycheck to Paycheck. *NBC News*. Retrieved from www.nbcnews.com/business/retirement/one-third-high-earners-are-living-paycheck-paycheck-n342726

INTERNAL REVENUE SERVICE. (2016). Free Tax Return Preparation for Qualifying Taxpayers. Retrieved from www.irs.gov/individuals/free-tax-return-preparation-for-you-by-volunteers

INTERNAL REVENUE SERVICE. (2016). IRS Announces 2017 Pension Plan Limitations; 401(k) Contribution Limit Remains Unchanged at $18,000 for 2017. Retrieved from www.irs.gov/uac/newsroom/irs-announces-2017-pension-plan-limitations-401k-contribution-limit-remains-unchanged-at-18000-for-2017.

INTERNAL REVENUE SERVICE. (2016). IRS Withholding Calculator. Retrieved from www.irs.gov/individuals/irs-withholding-calculator

INTERNAL REVENUE SERVICE. (2016). Qualifying Widow(er) with Dependent Child. *Filing Status*. Retrieved from www.irs.gov/publications/p17/ch02.html#en_US_2016_publink1000170830

INTERNAL REVENUE SERVICE. (2017). Earned Income Tax Credit
(EITC). Retrieved from www.irs.gov/credits-deductions/
individuals/earned-income-tax-credit

INTERNAL REVENUE SERVICE. (2017). Free File: Do Your Federal
Taxes for Free. Retrieved from www.irs.gov/uac/free-file-do-your-
federal-taxes-for-free

INTERNAL REVENUE SERVICE. (2017). Itemize or Choose the Standard
Deduction. Retrieved from www.irs.gov/uac/itemize-or-choose-
the-standard-deduction

INTERNAL REVENUE SERVICE. (2017). Payments. Retrieved from
www.irs.gov/payments

INTERNAL REVENUE SERVICE. (2017). Publication 530 - Main
Content. Retrieved from www.irs.gov/publications/p530/ar02.
html

INTERNAL REVENUE SERVICE. (2017). Topic 409 - Capital Gains and
Losses. Retrieved from www.irs.gov/taxtopics/tc409.html

INTERNAL REVENUE SERVICE. (2017). Topic 501 - Should I Itemize?
Retrieved from https://www.irs.gov/taxtopics/tc501.html

INTERNAL REVENUE SERVICE. (2017). Traditional and Roth IRAs.
Retrieved from www.irs.gov/retirement-plans/traditional-and-
roth-iras

INTUIT QUICKBOOKS. (2015). Intuit 2020 Report. Mountain View,
CA.

INVESTOPEDIA. (2017). Certified Financial Planner. *Terms*. Retrieved
from www.investopedia.com/terms/c/cfp.asp

INVESTOPEDIA. (2017). Certified Public Accountant - CPA. *Terms*.
Retrieved from www.investopedia.com/terms/c/cpa.asp

INVESTOPEDIA. (2017). Chartered Financial Analyst - CFA. *Terms.* Retrieved from www.investopedia.com/terms/c/cfa. asp#ixzz4mh3VSRml

INVESTOPEDIA. (2017). Chartered Financial Consultant - ChFC. *Terms.* Retrieved from www.investopedia.com/terms/c/ chartered-financial-consultant-chfc.asp#ixzz4mh3sa3aL

INVESTOPEDIA. (2017). Chartered Life Underwriter - CLU. *Terms.* Retrieved from www.investopedia.com/terms/c/clu. asp#ixzz4mh2Z3oll

INVESTOPEDIA. (2017). Enrolled Agent - EA. *Terms.* Retrieved from www.investopedia.com/terms/e/enrolled_agent.asp

INVESTOPEDIA. (2017). Registered Investment Advisor - RIA. *Terms.* Retrieved from www.investopedia.com/terms/r/ria. asp#ixzz4mh4I4D00

INVESTOPEDIA. (2017). Rule of 72. *Terms.* Retrieved from www.investopedia.com/terms/r/ruleof72.asp

KENNON, J. (2016). Warren Buffett Biography and the Evolution of Berkshire Hathaway. *The Balance.* Retrieved from https://www.thebalance.com/warren-buffett-biography-356436

KOBA, M. (2012). Facebook's IPO: What We Know Now. *CNBC.* Retrieved from www.cnbc.com/id/47043815

LANDSBAUM, C. (2015). Millennials Are the Most Educated, Worst Paid Generation. *Complex.* Retrieved from www.complex.com/pop-culture/2015/08/millennials-are-the-most-educated-worst-paid-generation

LANZA, A. (2016). Study: Student Loan Borrowers Delaying Other Life Decisions. *U.S. News.* Retrieved from www.usnews.com/ education/blogs/student-loan-ranger/articles/2016-01-20/study-student-loan-borrowers-delaying-other-life-decisions

LANZEN, M. (2013). Feeling Our Emotions. *Scientific American.* Retrieved from www.scientificamerican.com/article/feeling-our-emotions/

LARRIMORE, J., ARTHUR-BENTIL, M., DODINI, S., & THOMAS, L. (2015). Report on the Economic Well-Being of U.S. Households in 2014. Washington, DC: Federal Reserve Board.

LIST OF WEALTHIEST HISTORICAL FIGURES. (2017). Wikpiedia. Retrieved from http://en.wikipedia.org/wiki/List_of_wealthiest_historical_figures#Early_modern_to_modern_period

LUDWIG, S. (2012). Mark Zuckerberg Owns 28.2% of Facebook, Peter Thiel has 2.5%. *Venture Beat.* Retrieved from http://venturebeat.com/2012/02/01/facebook-s-1-zuckerberg-ownership/

MAC, R. (2012). How Much Facebook's Billionaires Are Worth Now That IPO Has Priced. *Forbes.* Retrieved from www.forbes.com/sites/ryanmac/2012/05/17/how-much-facebooks-billionaires-are-worth-now-that-ipo-has-priced/#7a88a7d6c6cf

MERLE, A. (2017). The Reading Habits of Ultra-Successful People. *The Huffington Post Blog.* Retrieved from www.huffingtonpost.com/andrew-merle/the-reading-habits-of-ult_b_9688130.html

MISCHEL, W. (2014). The Marshmallow Test: Mastering Self-Control. Boston, MA: Little, Brown and Company.

MORRISSEY, M. (2016). The State of American Retirement: How 401(k)s have failed most American Workers. *Retirement Inequality Chartbook.* Washington, DC: Economic Policy Institute.

MORTGAGE CALCULATOR. (2017). Retrieved from www.mortgagecalculator.org

MORTGAGE CALCULATOR. (2017). Extra Mortgage Payment Calculator. Retrieved from www.mortgagecalculator.org/calculators/what-if-i-pay-more-calculator.php

ORAN, O., & BARR, A. (2012). Facebook prices at top of range in landmark IPO. *Reuters.* Retrieved from www.reuters.com/article/us-facebook-idUSBRE84G14Q20120517

PAUL, K. (2017). $1 billion in gift cards go unused every year — here's how to avoid that. *MarketWatch.* Retrieved from http://www.marketwatch.com/story/1-billion-in-gift-cards-go-unused-every-year-heres-how-to-avoid-that-2016-12-30

PORTER'S FIVE FORCES ANALYSIS. (2017). Wikipedia. Retrieved from http://en.wikipedia.org/wiki/Porter%27s_five_forces_analysis

PEPITONE, J. (2013). Marissa Mayer's biggest Yahoo buy is 75% cool factor. *CNN Tech.* Retrieved from http://money.cnn.com/2013/08/09/technology/yahoo-tumblr-goodwill/index.html

PEST ANALYSIS. (2017). Wikpiedia. Retrieved from http://en.wikipedia.org/wiki/PEST_analysis

SCHENKE, J. (2014). Only 1 in 3 college students getting key work experience they need, according to survey. *Purdue University News.* Retrieved from http://purdue.edu/newsroom/releases/2014/Q4/only-1-in-3-college-students-getting-key-work-experience-they-need,-according-to-survey.html

STRAUSS, K. (2016). These Are The Skills Bosses Say New College Grads Do Not Have. *Forbes.* Retrieved from www.forbes.com/sites/karstenstrauss/2016/05/17/these-are-the-skills-bosses-say-new-college-grads-do-not-have/#31cbc1945491

SUN, W. (2015). 7 Frightening Millennial Money Trends. *Forbes.* Retrieved from www.forbes.com/sites/winniesun/2015/10/30/halloweenmillennials/#1d3db8b04601

SZALAY, J. (2017). Giant Sequoias and Redwoods: The Largest and Tallest Trees. *Live Science.* Retrieved from www.livescience.com/39461-sequoias-redwood-trees.html

SWOT ANALYSIS. (2017). Wikpiedia. Retrieved from
   http://en.wikipedia.org/wiki/SWOT_analysis

THE ASSOCIATED PRESS. (2007). Microsoft Invests $240 Million
   in Facebook. NBC News. Retrieved from www.nbcnews.com/
   id/21458486/ns/business-us_business/t/microsoft-invests-million-
   facebook/#.WX4IEojyvIV

U.S. SMALL BUSINESS ADMINISTRATION. (2017). Borrowing Money for
   Your Business. *Starting a Business.* Retrieved from
   www.sba.gov/starting-business/business-financials/borrowing-
   money-your-business

UNITED STATES CENSUS BUREAU. (2014). Where is the Wealth?
   - Median Household Net Worth by Quintile. *Infographics
   & Visualizations.* Retrieved from https://census.gov/library/
   visualizations/2014/comm/cb14-156_net_worth.html

UNITED STATES SECURITIES AND EXCHANGE COMMISSION. (2017).
   Annuities. *Introduction to Investing.* Retrieved from https://
   investor.gov/introduction-investing/basics/investment-products/
   annuities

UNITED STATES SECURITIES AND EXCHANGE COMMISSION. (2017).
   Bonds. *Introduction to Investing.* Retrieved from https://investor.
   gov/introduction-investing/basics/investment-products/bonds

UNITED STATES SECURITIES AND EXCHANGE COMMISSION. (2017).
   Commodities. *Introduction to Investing.* Retrieved from
   https://investor.gov/introduction-investing/basics/investment-
   products/commodities

UNITED STATES SECURITIES AND EXCHANGE COMMISSION. (2017).
   Exchange Traded Funds (ETFs). *Introduction to Investing.*
   Retrieved from https://investor.gov/introduction-investing/basics/
   investment-products/exchange-traded-funds-etfs

UNITED STATES SECURITIES AND EXCHANGE COMMISSION. (2017).
   Municipal Bonds. *Introduction to Investing.* Retrieved from

https://investor.gov/introduction-investing/basics/investment-products/municipal-bonds

UNITED STATES SECURITIES AND EXCHANGE COMMISSION. (2017).
Mutual Funds. *Introduction to Investing.* Retrieved from
https://investor.gov/investing-basics/investment-products/mutual-funds

UNITED STATES SECURITIES AND EXCHANGE COMMISSION. (2017).
Real Estate Investment Trusts (REITS). *Introduction to Investing.*
Retrieved from http://investor.gov/introduction-investing/basics/investment-products/real-estate-investment-trusts-reits

UNITED STATES SECURITIES AND EXCHANGE COMMISSION. (2017). Saving
For Education - 529 Plans. *Introduction to Investing.* Retrieved
from http://investor.gov/introduction-investing/basics/investment-products/saving-education-529-plans

UNITED STATES SECURITIES AND EXCHANGE COMMISSION. (2017).
Stocks. *Introduction to Investing.* Retrieved from https://investor.gov/introduction-investing/basics/investment-products/stocks

VALUEINVESTINGPRO. (2009). Warren Buffet on Ben Graham: YouTube.
Retrieved from www.youtube.com/watch?v=HCZMs01W0KM

WEATHERSPOON, C. P. (1990). Giant Sequoia. In R. M. Burns & B.
H. Honkala (Eds.), *Silvics of North America* (Vol. 1). Washington,
DC: U.S. Department of Agriculture Forest Service. Retrieved
from https://www.na.fs.fed.us/spfo/pubs/silvics_manual/Volume_1/sequoiadendron/giganteum.htm